Against the Odds

A Path Forward for Rural America

By Bruce Vincent,

Nicole J Olynk Widmar

and Jessica Eise

D1417126

Cover design: Jessica Eise and Thilo Balke

ISBN-13: 978-1544035307
ISBN-10: 1544035306

This book is dedicated to my family. Those who moved west to settle, those who helped raise me and those with whom I was raised. Of special note in that family tree is the most awesome mate on earth, PJ, and my children: Chas, Echo Jo, Lacie and Vance. They have lived this journey with me and make life worth living.

-Bruce

How to read this unique book

This book is the result of a collaboration by an unlikely trio, namely a logger (Bruce Vincent), an associate professor (Nicole Olynk Widmar) and a journalist (Jessica Eise). Bruce and Nicole met presenting back-to-back at an agricultural conference and instantly recognized the potential in aligning their messages. Jessica was invited onboard to round out the team with literary and journalistic expertise.

The result of this unique collaboration is, you could say, an annotated life story around the experiences of Bruce Vincent. Context, examples and additions are peppered throughout to help translate Bruce's stories and to connect them, often quite frankly and directly, to other happenings across agriculture, current events of the day and ongoing social science research.

It is our hope that you read this story and, apart from living the heartache, anxiety and hope of the people of Vincent Logging and Libby, you consider the potential for applying the lessons learned in logging to other sectors, or even your own personal relationships.

By no means is this book the final word, nor presented as the ultimate truth. This is simply one man's story placed in broader context, written and shared with the intent and hope of facilitating progress around social issues, particularly those centered around the management of our natural resources.

It is through stories that we learn, and through the sharing of our stories that we help others understand us. We don't have to achieve consensus to facilitate progress, but we must hear one another. If a person is just another tally on a spreadsheet of 'impacted others,' we easily fail to appreciate the ramifications of lost livelihoods, broken communities or a mismanaged cause. The power of a story lies in its ability to humanize and lend insight into someone else's reality. Be warmed by the perseverance of Bruce and his family, yet also consider your own ability to move the needle and facilitate progress.

Table of Contents

Part One

A Rural American

Preface: The Iowa Basics

Back when I was a kid, third graders in our rural school were subjected to the Iowa Basics tests. Administered to students across the country, it was the test that would, allegedly, tell you just how smart or dumb you were. I was horrified at the prospect of taking them, but did the best I could.

When the results came back, the school principal and my teacher called Mom and Dad. 'Can you come in for a meeting at school?' they asked.

I was supposed to go to bed and sleep while my parents talked. Naturally, like any nervous eight-year old under those circumstances, I did not. The principal and teacher had called Dad and Mom into school, and all that could mean was that life as I knew it was coming to a screeching halt. Whatever the news, it was certainly not good.

As I lay awake waiting for the folks to return, my third-grade stomach churned. I tossed and turned, sweaty and nervous. When they finally got back, I pressed my ear against the thin walls of our mobile home. My folks thought I was sleeping. But with my fear-heightened senses, I could hear every single word they said. And those words carried with them a damning message that neither my father, mother nor I really understood at the time.

It was a message being shared in rural homes all over the country. And to a certain extent, it still is shared today. 'How do we keep Bruce from becoming a logger?'

The message of the well-intentioned principal and teacher was just as clear as it was weighted: Bruce had scored high on the Iowa Basics test. If he ended up being a logger, it was Dad's fault. Another message though, one being sent only too clearly, was that Bruce was too smart to be a dumb ol' logger like his dad.

While they talked in our small living room, I could hear the confusion in Dad's voice. He was trying to figure out how to keep me from being like himself. He did not know what to do. They talked about getting me a library card (which they did), they talked about getting me a desk to shove into my tiny room (which they did and which I still have) and they talked about trying to save money so I could go to college someday (they took out a whole life insurance policy that would grow with me and pay for some college in time). And with a growing clump of four young boys, that was the best they could do.

It was with this unspoken backdrop that I graduated as a Libby Logger from Libby Senior High School. I left a bunch of world-class friends, whom I still get to bother on a daily basis in my adult life, and headed for college. Much later, after finishing college and beginning my own family, I was able to look back on this evening and finally understand the full impact it had on Mom and Dad, and millions like them over the course of decades. I am sure that it was the first time in my proud father's life he looked down at his hands without a feeling of pride at the hard-won callouses on his palms and the dirt under his fingernails. I am sure that it was the first time that his hands and his hard work were instead a source of shame and guilt for both he and Mom.

But it was those hands that built our family company and hands like his that built our towns, our state and our whole dang country. Yet Mom and Dad, and millions like them, got the very clear message that they did not have a heritage worthy of passing on, at least not to intelligent children. So they wrapped that misplaced mantle of shame and guilt around their necks and quietly wore it for decades.

They were proud that I scored high on the tests but knew that it was their 'job' to make sure that I 'bettered' myself by not growing up to be like them. My path away from the family heritage, the culture I loved and the business I was proud to be a part of was polluted with a perverse mixture of shame and pride.

My father did not know that I had overheard his and Mom's conversation that night. It was nearly thirty years later, and after I had moved back home, when he heard me share the story from a podium as he sat with an audience of 5,000 similar souls at a Cowboy and Logger celebration in Missoula. He sobbed for nearly an hour.

I pray that real healing of his inner self was what brought the tears that day. I pray that he knows that he and Mom did not let me down nor did they fail my three incredibly intelligent brothers who, after leaving home, also returned and chose to be loggers. They gave us the foundation of a life worth living and a heritage for which we are all eternally proud. I pray that when we buried him in 2011, the one thing missing in his grave was that damned mantle of guilt.

I have spent the better part of my adult life attempting to rip this misplaced mantle of guilt from those unfortunate enough to have knowingly or unknowingly slipped it over their heads. I was lucky enough to be able to eventually come home and work with Dad and my brothers in the forests I love. I was lucky enough to stand by them as we studied the rolling hillsides covered in the public's trees, figuring out how to most sensitively apply modern forest management. I was also astute enough to know that while I stood there with a high school diploma and two college degrees hanging on my wall, and my father had not even one, the less intelligent of the two was not my father.

Chapter 1: A Family of the West

For a young boy such as myself, who loved the out-of-doors, growing up in Libby, Montana, was idyllic. As the second in a line of four sons, life was good. Like water from a fire hose, the refrain of, 'Billy (Will), Bruce, Steve, Scott!' rolled off the tongues of family, friends and neighbors as they rounded us up for an event or, in many cases, a comeuppance for some sort of mischievous endeavor or another.

My forefathers and mothers, like many families of that time in the West, moved around as they sought to scrape a living out of a rapidly-changing landscape. We didn't find our way to Libby until my parents, soon after their marriage, moved out to Montana where I was raised and still live. Yet my maternal and paternal grandparents and great-grandparents were an integral part of the fabric of rural life in the West.

Dad, the first child of Bill and Hazel Vincent, was born in Thompson Falls, Montana, in 1934. His mid-depression upbringing in a timber, ranching and farming family was tough by today's standards, but I never heard a negative word or complaint about his early days. He went to school, enjoyed sports, played the trumpet in band and proudly operated a paper route in his town of 1,000 souls.

Yet it wasn't all so picturesque. Issues constantly arose due to the actions of his brilliant but alcoholic father. These issues frequently evolved into problems that my dad, despite his young age, had to resolve on his own. Yet Grandpa 'Poo,' as we called him, could transform a complex idea like a sawmill into reality without ever using a blueprint. A master carpenter and mechanical genius, Poo was amazing – when he was sober.

He and his brother, my Uncle Bob, built logging companies and sawmills. Through this they provided a nice middle-income existence for the families involved. However, every so often, Poo would take off on what we called a 'bender' or a 'running drunk.' The bender might go on for a few days, weeks or even months before Poo would come home to 'dry out.' Six months, a year or even two or three years of brilliantly navigating the tough economic times facing his family during the hard years of the Great Depression would inevitably come crashing down in a matter of weeks.

The rebuilding of both human and business relationships would commence when Poo returned home. Dad was joined there over time by three sisters, Patty, Robin and Echo. Yet the glue that held the family unit together was a combination of my Grandma Hazel, who had a series of jobs to keep food on the table when Poo was not around, and Dad as the eldest son. During Dad's junior year of high school, Poo relocated the family to Yreka, California, to build a mill and forge a new start. Dad entered high school in Yreka with a goal of finishing his schooling, but not all of his Montana classes had transferred. He was one class short when it came time to walk with his class. He could have stayed for another semester, but his responsibilities as the oldest child overtook his need for a high school diploma when Poo went on yet another bender. Dad never managed to get his diploma.

To help care for the family and begin to build his life, Dad got a job with a construction company working on a new highway running from Seattle to Los Angeles. He yearned for his home back in Montana, but needed to make a living that would take care of not just his needs but those of the family. So he focused on construction for a few years. It was during this time that he and my Mom met on a sidewalk in the little town of Oakland, Oregon. At 19-years old, Dad was driving through this small town when he noticed the pretty 15-year old girl drop a sack of groceries she was lugging home from the store as part of her family chores. Smitten, Dad struck up a conversation with Mom, and they began a courtship that lasted over 40 years.

Mom's family had just recently moved to western Oregon from their home in Harney County, Oregon. Named after her Great Grandma, Julia Ann Hayes, Mom was born in Burns, Oregon, in 1938. Mom's namesake, Julia Ann Hayes, came to eastern Oregon on the Oregon Trail in 1856. Today, she is known as the 'Pioneer Mother' of Harney County.

The hardscrabble existence on the high desert was not suited for the weak at heart. Native Americans shared the space and were rambunctious and rightfully angry as they were paraded off the landscape many still claimed as their home. There wasn't always a clear rule of law, and self-sufficiency was mandatory. My pipe-smoking, gun-toting great, great grandma Julia was up to the challenge and she and her husband Cyrus raised their children on the new frontier.

Her granddaughter, my grandma Merle Kendall, was born in 1906. With her three brothers, they cut hay with teams of horses, tended to the cattle and sheep and wove the industrial revolution's tools of farming and ranching into the fabric of their homestead. She was largely raised by her brothers. She was the youngest and lost her mother to breast cancer when she was just six, and only a few years later lost her father to lockjaw from an infected tooth.

Despite these challenges, Grandma Merle was enjoying her young adulthood as a roaring 1920s flapper in a small, isolated high desert ranch town of Burns when she met a cowboy that stole her heart. His name was Lute. Born to a pioneering family while wagon-training through Nebraska on their way to Montana in 1900, Grandpa Lute Kendall was among the last of the wild-west's bronc busters. Grandpa Lute started school in Plains, Montana, just over the Cabinet Mountains from Libby. His father ran mule trains of supplies to the many small mining encampments scattered around the southern edges of the snowcapped mountain range. When highways and railroads removed the need for those services, he moved the family to eastern Oregon where he ran supply trains between Nevada and the outback ranches of Eastern Oregon.

As a strapping young man, my Grandpa and future mentor Lute found that he had an affinity for the process of breaking and training the wild horses that were captured and used as ranching stock by the area's ranchers. As a young 'buckaroo' he traveled from ranch to ranch providing his services. In the early 1920s, Lute was discovered by a very rich older lady from Portland. She scooped him up, took him to Portland, dressed him in quite natty city clothes from the fancy Nordstrom's downtown store and paid him to be her personal chauffeur.

As I'm built just like my Grandpa Lute, those wonderful old gangster-style suits of the era still fit and I've worn them off and on over the years. I have also seen pictures of the young Eastern Oregon stud and lady for whom he worked, and think Grandpa might have been being paid for more than driving her car. Although I could never get him to affirm my suspicions, I did learn upon eager questioning that a 'gentlemen never talks.' One of many life lessons gained from a wise and truly gentle man.

Despite his nice set-up, Grandpa Lute did not like the city life much. So after a few short years he headed back to his passion, the ranchlands and ranch culture of eastern Oregon. Now a seasoned hand, he was no longer bronc-busting but made a living managing ranches owned by others. On a visit to a barn dance in Burns, he met a young and vivacious flapper from a ranch family with deep roots in the area, my very own Grandma Merle Hayes. They soon eloped to Winnemucca, Nevada, and were married. He and Grandma Merle had two children, my Uncle Allen Kendall and my Mom, Julia.

When Mom was born, Grandpa Lute was foreman of the White Horse Ranch south of Burns. The owners of the White

Horse Ranch sold out (the ranch is now a national monument), so Grandpa Lute and his family headed to western Oregon. Grandpa Lute and a few of his brothers began working for logging companies in the area as truck drivers. It was there, while he was working 'in the woods' and living in Oakland, Oregon, where a young Montanan spotted Lute and Merle's daughter, Julia, and her spilled bag of groceries on the little town's sidewalk.

Soon, they were married. And, after chasing road construction jobs in Oregon, they returned to Montana and settled in Libby. My Dad was the income generator of the family unit. Mom was the homemaker. Dad went to work each day before daylight graced the heat-holding window curtains of our small mobile home. Most folks today are familiar with the HGTV heralded fad of 'tiny home' living, but in our world it was not a television-making fad. It was simply our reality.

Two parents and four boys were stacked into a two bedroom, one bath, 10' by 55' New Moon mobile home with a 150 square foot 'lean-to' added on for additional room. It was our castle and Mom, a clean freak in the eyes of us boys, made it our home. It was also an improvement over the 8' by 32' Nashua mobile home we lived in for years before the third child was born. That home was also 'our castle,' but had some drawbacks, like when the sheets froze to the walls in the frigid winters of the late 1950s and early 1960s.

My early life in Libby, and the history of my family, aren't anything uncommon for a rural family of the west. In the early 1900s Great Grandad Vincent, a civil engineer, helped lay out the town of Polson, Montana, while Great Grandma Vincent concentrated on building the social fabric of town by starting book clubs and theatre groups. Some in the family (on both sides) pursued cattle ranching, some dabbled in mining and others delved into forest management. In hindsight, our upbringing was typical for rural resource families of the time. It was a rugged landscape full of tough, strong and resilient characters.

Chapter 2: Libby, Montana

Libby is a small town in Montana. It's hard to get to. No airports are terribly close. And it's one of the most beautiful places in the world. Libby is my home. It's where my father began logging and where I was fortunate enough to have worked with him and my brothers.

Where my town currently stands was, at one time, a giant sheet of ice. Some 10,000 years ago, that ice-cap receded after 100,000 years of a glacial age. Native Americans moved into the land mass being evacuated by the ice. Following the receding ice-cap, they launched what is now a several thousand-year regime of human influence. The plains and mountain areas were regenerating with grasses and forests, and Native Americans were able to utilize the area for harvesting of their food supplies.

These nomadic hunter-gatherers of the Kootenai/Salish tribe traversed the mountainous area in search of food. It was not welcoming country and largely unfit for yearlong habitation. Yet it served as a fruitful travel-way between the more temperate areas of the Okanagan, Elk and Flathead valleys to the northwest and south. The most welcoming area of what is now Lincoln

County was in the northeast, near what is now the town of Eureka. Eureka is in the center of the Tobacco Valley, which was so named as it provided enough of a growing season to allow the natives to grow tobacco while they rummaged the surrounding forestlands for the deer, elk, moose and other game.

The Kootenai River winds south from the Canadian border through Eureka and onward to the heart of the county. While a fairly deep, slow-moving and lazy river in the north of the county, the river chokes into tight chasms of rapids and spectacular waterfalls as it cuts its way through the Cabinet Range portion of the Purcell Mountains in south Lincoln County. The tightening of the river valley begins near Libby and extends through to the Idaho line. The ease of lazy river travel ends just north of Libby and while stunningly beautiful, the rough rapids served as an impediment to travel. It contributed to the isolation of the area during Native American habitation, an isolation that continued after European settlers attempted to settle the northwest.

In this mountainous region, tree cover was not a friend of the Native Americans. Too many trees and too much brush made it difficult to travel through the area. It also made it difficult to see both their prey and enemies. They sought to improve both the travel and hunting features of the forestlands by using the management tool most commonly utilized by these early settlers throughout the North American continent – fire.

According to bog and tree ring analysis, Native Americans travelled through the Libby area every ten to twelve years for a millennium. After utilizing all that they could from the forest, they would set fire to the landscape. The fires served many purposes, with the most important being the removal of the brush and small trees that hampered travel and impeded their line-of-sight while seeking prey or avoiding two-legged enemies. It also, they learned, invigorated the topsoil and improved the growth of the grasses and other forage that their prey depended upon for survival.

Native Americans were practicing forest management for thousands of years before European settlers first wandered in.

When these explorers and settlers did arrive, they found a beautiful landscape that had been defined by fire; both intentionally set and naturally occurring. The forest was dominated by stands of timber in the valley bottoms that included somewhere around 50 or 60 thick-barked, fire resistant trees per acre. The berries were abundant, the grass was deep and the ungulates the natives consumed and shared with the predator population thrived.

Early writings by explorers such as David Thompson, in the very early 1800s, spoke of a forest composition that was a mix of unbearably thick stands of lodge pole pine interspersed with stands of huge, thick-barked, fire resistant ponderosa pine, western larch and Douglas fir. Wetter areas in this moisture rich section of Montana were populated by stands of hemlock, cedar and softwoods, often seen in the rainforest areas closer to the Pacific Coast. Many of the forest observers also noted the evidence of fire throughout the area, although they mistakenly thought of the fire 'scars' as being caused strictly by naturally-occurring fires wrought by dry summer lightning.

These early writings by European explorers marked the advancement of other European settlers into the area in search of highly prized beaver pelts for the largely London-based fur trade. An accompanying and complicating factor that visited the area with the early explorers, however, was disease. These diseases attacked the immune systems of entire populations of indigenous people. By the mid-1800s, small pox, hepatitis, measles and other Euro-centric diseases decimated the populations that preexisted European settlement. Strained and often violent relations with the colonizing Europeans emerged. The nomadic hunting regimes of the Native Americans ended during this time period.

By the late 1800s, the Native Americans had been relegated to isolated pockets of stationary communities on reservations. Their removal from the landscape also removed their management by fire from the forest base, with dire consequences. Their thousands of years old eco-management was erased.

During this time, the organic matter that had historically been removed by Native American-managed fires began to accumulate into what is called, in modern parlance, 'forest fire fuel loading.' Trees that, under the historic management regime, would have been killed by intermittent fire when but a few feet tall were now allowed to grow into full-sized trees. Brush that would have been removed by those same intermittent fires now produced a mat of organic matter. The tops of the trees grew so close together they provided a natural 'canopy' of cover blocking sunlight from reaching the forest floor and impeding the growth of berry bushes and grasses.

In the Libby area, the decimation of Native American populations correlated with the arrival of a new breed of European settler in search of mineral values in the rock formations of the Purcell Mountains. Early miners found the geology of the area offered great finds of silver, copper and gold. But the area was isolated and offered no easy access from any direction.

As the gold rush in California came to an end, those seeking the next mother lode, and not afraid of the isolation of the mountains of northwest Montana, finagled their way into the high valleys panning for signs of embedded riches in the stream courses. Clusters of wealth-seeking pioneers coagulated into numerous tiny bergs scattered across the landscape. Named after a miner's daughter, the town of Libby formed in the upper reaches of Libby Creek. Timber was harvested as needed to provide logs for cabins and shoring timber for mine shafts. Yet while there were many small finds, only a few struck it rich.

In the late 1880s, the Burlington Northern Railroad chose a route along the Kootenai River as a crossing for the intercontinental route connecting Minneapolis to Seattle. The previous impediments to travel and settlement presented by river rapids and falls were sidestepped by the rail line. The connection to the outer world no longer depended solely upon the small ferry system in the upper Kootenai reaches and the mule trains coming over the southern Cabinet Mountains from the growing Silver Valley complex.

When a train stop was put in place near the confluence of Libby Creek and the Kootenai River, the miners of the Libby Creek area relocated their center of business from the upper mountain valley to the rail line in the valley bottom. The rail line introduced, for the first time, the ability to market the timber resources. The line also made mining of the newly discovered vermiculite just northeast of the new Libby site economically viable. To this day, decades of mining this asbestos-laced material, before the health hazards of asbestos were fully understood, continues to impact many of the mineworkers and their families. The Libby area is now labeled a Super Fund Site and clean up from the now closed facility remains ongoing.

Milling of the areas' forests for outside consumption facilitated growth of a logging and milling infrastructure that soon overshadowed the small mining operations, in both size and scope of business. The Libby area's previous economic foundation, built solely upon mining, was now complemented by the production and export of timber. The Bonners Ferry Lumber Company built a sawmilling complex in Libby and built the transportation systems needed to move the raw logs from the treasury of forestlands into the mill for value-added breakdown into useable products for a growing nation. Logging became the backbone of Libby's economy.

In the late 1800s and early 1900s, the vast majority of forest management took place on private industrial lands. Concerned that the lands of the west previously open to homesteading could be abused, the federal government, under President Grover Cleveland, sought to protect some of these from short-term commercial exploitation. This federal land ultimately became the foundation for the formation of federal bureaucracies such as of the Bureau of Land Management, United States Forest Service (USFS) and National Park Service. In many places in the west, like Lincoln County, Montana, nearly 80 percent of the land within the county is under federal management.

The timber barons fought this move, fearful of the devaluation of their private timber holdings. The USFS worked hard to convince the timber owners that they were not going to glut the market. The USFS did not aggressively manage the public land-holdings at first, spending most of their time on inventory, trail management and firefighting. It wasn't until the post WWII era that management began in earnest, and by this time private industrial landowners welcomed the inclusion of the federal base into their mill sustainability formulas. Industry needed the federal land timber flow to feed the mouths of the mills.

In the early 1900s, the J. Neils family bought the lands of the Bonners Ferry Lumber Company, who believed there were no holdings worth going after beyond that first entry. Yet as it turned out, the J. Neils family was the true timber baron. Their at-the-time socially acceptable method of forest management was buying forestlands, summarily stripping them of timber value and searching for the next patch of timbered land to 'manage.' Like many other natural resource management cultures, the human need to 'subdue' the wilderness and 'carve' out a space for the human species overtook any fledgling concern about environmental impacts – either short or long term. Society as a whole was so busy taking care of immediate needs like food, clothing and shelter that the secondary issues of environmental impacts just had not (yet) risen to real concern for the vast majority of the population.

The Neils' last stop before coming to Libby was in the Bemidji/Caste Lake area of northern Minnesota. The Great Northern Railroad had been completed and, when they purchased the lands around Libby, they loaded their workers, their workers' families and the milling infrastructure on the railroad and off-loaded in their new home. The J. Neils' Lumber Company purchased private industrial lands from the Anaconda Company and built a milling complex in both Libby and the neighboring small town of Troy. The timber culture of the area nestled in right alongside the historic mining camps still dotting the area.

The logging and milling businesses in the area ultimately employed around 2,000 men and women. The Neils family, recognizing that there were no new forest lands to 'subdue' in the old method of 'cut-and-run,' developed a two-hundred-year forest sustainability plan that included reforestation techniques still studied by the World Commission of Forestry. In doing so, they provided an economic and cultural heartbeat for the area, one that survived the depression era and thrived through the late 1940s to the 1960s. It was into this environment that I was born and spent my young years.

Chapter 3: Growing Up & Moving Out

My life changed in third grade after the Iowa Basics results were shared with Mom and Dad. I focused on my studies through the rest of my schooling in Libby. This was not that hard, really, since I was very small. In fact, when I entered high school, I was 4' 10" and hoping I wouldn't have to join the circus to get a job.

Luckily, I did not. I started work at the local tire shop, owned by our neighbor Jack Coup, when I was 12. I enjoyed getting tips from the customers when the 'little guy' wrestled the logging truck tires. The tips helped supplement the 65 cents an hour minimum wage. I also did what all others in the area did, helping put up hay on area ranches. On weekends, I also worked for Vincent Logging doing odd jobs like digging the snow from around the base of trees for 5 cents a stump, which enabled our wintertime sawyers to reach the bottoms of the trees they were going to fell. Not to mention, I pulled weeds in neighbors' gardens and delivered the weekly *Grit* newspaper by horseback.

Dad taught me to not cause fights on the playground or in the halls of school. Yet he also assured me that, if I should find myself in a fight, I had better make the first swing count because I may not get a second one. So I joined the local boxing group to learn how to fight, or at least take a good solitary swing. This advice served me well. Since I was little I had no patience for bullying and my fights in school generally amounted to me taking a good first swing and then getting the snot beat out of me. The upside to the strategy was that the bullies avoided my friends and me, because I did learn to stick swing number one.

Being of tiny stature, I didn't really have a shot at organized public school sports until my last two years of high school. But I did get involved in student government and served as class president through middle and high school.

When I finally grew, it was awesome. In the spring of my sophomore year, I sprouted from 4' 10" to my current 5'10" by July. I grew so fast, in fact, that my cartilage couldn't keep up with my bone growth so I had to wear braces on my arms. It hurt so, so good. Being a bit bigger, I was finally able to play football during my junior and senior years. Football made it legal to smack around some of the guys I had wanted to smack around for ten years.

After graduating, I left for my predetermined destiny – college. I was the first in several generations of my immediate family to graduate from high school and the first to attend college. I knew nothing about the process. But cousin Rob Vincent from Oregon spent summers in Montana with us and he was headed to MT. Hood Community College in Gresham, Oregon, so I joined him. Dad's cousin from Thompson Falls was an auto tech professor at the same school, so I had some family ties helping to pave my way.

I was 17 when I moved to Oregon for the summer to establish residency in order to afford tuition. My major was political science. I was going to be a politician and work to assist the folks from the rural area I had left. I got involved in student government the first week of college and was elected to the student council. I learned some valuable lessons during those early years, principally that change can be generated when people, who are in minority situations, stand together and become the 'swing vote' that defines election results.

In the spring of 1975, I was serving as student president of the college. As such, I was also a member of the Student Presidents Association. Chosen to represent the students of Oregon at the annual Student Fly-In to Washington, DC, I boarded the plane for our nation's capital armed with great intentions and reams of information on 53 pieces of legislation that students across America were supporting. While the student groups were pushing for passage of all 53 bills there were, in my eyes, only three that had merit. The others were really only perks that would cost millions of taxpayer dollars. Since the timber industry was in a recession at the time, I knew that my tax-paying family in Montana could ill afford any pork-filled bills.

After two intense days of strategizing in a DC hotel, several hundred student leaders hit the Hill. We were each armed with two sheets of paper. On one we had a bulleted listing of the bills we supported. On the other was a listing of every senator and representative and two columns of numbers. The first column displayed the winning margin of the last election for the given senator or representative. The second column listed the number of students (read: potential voters) in that person's district or state. In every case, the number of students (read: potential voters) was larger than the previous winning margin.

While visiting with the staff members of those I was assigned to harangue, I grew increasingly alarmed at how the system worked. It was really quite simple. I met with staffers, handed them the list of supported legislation and pointed out the margin of victory and student population. Very, very little time was then spent on discussing the merits of the bills. A great deal of time was spent discussing the mood of the students (read: potential voters). Remember, in 1975, the memory of student rebellions was fresh on many leaders' minds.

The question that was never directly asked was, "Do you want us angry at your boss?" While unsaid, it was certainly not unheard. We passed all 53 pieces of legislation. Clearly afraid of the 'swing' vote potential, the politicians acted in the best interest of themselves…. err, the country. Disillusioned, I returned to

Oregon, quit school, dropped my major of political science and vowed to never enter politics again unless it was from a ground-based position of reality. I'm afraid we are still paying for some of the pork that I helped pass. In my own defense, it was from a place of good intentions and we've since learned much about the potential impacts of unbridled good intentions.

After leaving MT. Hood Community College, I came back to Montana to log with the family company for a year. Really I came back to reconsider my life path. I wanted to return to my home. I wanted to have a career that made it possible to live in Montana. Yet I knew the mantle of guilt being worn by my father if I chose to return to logging, so I begrudgingly took that option off of the table. I worked as a sawyer (the guy who whacks down the trees with a chainsaw) and pondered my future.

During the summer of 1975, I lost my Grandpa Lute. He told the family he was going to plant asparagus in our garden and make the darn stuff grow if it was the last thing he did. On that early morning in June, we saw him walk from his house to the garden spot with an armload of asparagus roots. An hour later he returned to his home, lay down and suffered a life ending heart attack. Hearing Grandma Merle's screams, we all converged on Grandpa's bedroom and I broke several of his ribs trying to bring my mentor back to life. It was not to be. He was 75. He had lived a full and gratifying life. We had to let him go and find peace in knowing we got to share in that life. I miss him to this day.

Shortly after Grandpa Lute passed, I took a spin on a thinning crew. Thinning crews fall the little trees in an area to allow the other trees to prosper. It is back-breaking work but necessary to keep the forest healthy. We were camped in tents about 45 miles north of Libby in the middle of the Yaak area. Our encampment was very close to absolutely nothing. So after spending a few weeks in camp, we got our first paychecks and rushed to town on a Friday night to cash those checks and share our earnings with a bar.

There was live music at a local bar, The Mine, so some friends and I headed there to spread our wealth around. When I walked into the bar, I was greeted by someone, I was not sure by whom, but it was a girl. And she wrapped her arms around my neck. Looking down, all I could see was long, blonde hair cascading down to her waist, a tube top and a tan.

I thought jokingly to myself, 'I don't know who you are, but I think I want you to be my wife.' As she pulled away, I recognized her at once as Patti Jo Dahl. Patti Jo was the Californian cousin of a friend from a neighboring ranch near ours. I had met her twice before and, though the first visit had not gone well, the second visit ended in a kissing marathon in the closet of my bedroom. Yeehaw! I thought. Her graduation present from her parents was a trip to the place she loved most on earth. Libby, Montana.

Our first meeting, the one that hadn't gone well, was some six years earlier when I was 12 and Patti Jo was 11. She and her cousin came to visit at our place. I was sporting a crew cut and bib overalls. She was wearing fingernail polish and no bib overalls. My brothers, friends and a few neighbor kids were thick in the middle of a horse turd war centered upon our three-storied fort in the horse pasture. Excited to have a newcomer, we offered Patti Jo the top floor of the fort (bottom floors had issues with wafting debris from above) and even offered her dry turds for the fight. She declined our offer, and I was certain that I would never like the uppity Californian with finger nail polish who was too good to play with us.

The second meeting went better. By then I was 16 and she was 15. We went to the drive-in theater and sat on swings watching 'Love Story' and talked. And talked. Oh, and we kissed. Then she went back to California.

It was that third meeting at The Mine that changed the course of my life. That time when Patti Jo (PJ) went back to California, she took my heart with her. After weeks of moping around the house and the job, Dad finally told me that I had better do something about connecting with that California girl or my long face was going to be permanently dragging on the floor. So I phoned her at her job working at a donut shop in San Jose, California, and the rest is history.

We married in Libby on August 7, 1976. Soon after we left for college together with all of the money I had earned logging. We had a small U-Haul full of our meager belongings and big dreams for our life ahead. I re-entered college in the civil engineering program, hoping that with an engineering degree I would be able to one day make it back to Montana. PJ enrolled in medical secretary classes, determined to one day get her nursing degree.

Two weeks after deciding we would wait to start a family until we were both done with college, well, life happened. We took a pregnancy test and it was positive. We were both elated and scared to death. We were young, we were broke and we were barely getting started. Soothed by Mom's lifelong saying that 'there is always room for another baby,' we embraced our new path and began preparing to be parents. PJ worked at a Portland hospital while she was puking her way through pregnancy. I went to school while working as the school mascot for $5 an hour. I served as a bouncer for the local college theater productions. I sold Cutco Cutlery door to door. And we built the foundation for a marriage that has now thrived for over forty years.

I left college early the first year since PJ was about to deliver our firstborn. We had no health insurance so we needed to be in Montana and making some serious money logging. Chas arrived on July 24, 1977. I had hoped for July 7, giving him the honor of being born on 7-7-77, with plans of naming him Sven. But I got shot down on all counts. I did cut my arm with a chain saw on the 7th of July and ended up at the doctor (not PJ). Oh, well.

We returned to Portland where I finished my associate degree in Civil Engineering Technology and moved to Spokane, Washington, to enroll at Gonzaga University to finish my bachelors in engineering. While in school at Gonzaga, I worked weekends logging in Montana (some 3.5 hours away) and finally secured a job as a central service tech at Deaconess Medical Center to gain insurance coverage for our growing family. PJ started a daycare in our home and we enjoyed up to 12 little urchins a day running around our tiny house. In 1980, we welcomed into our home our first daughter, Echo Jo. Our third child, Lacie, joined us in 1983 after I had at long last completed my studies at Gonzaga with a bachelor of science in Civil Engineering and a master's in Business Administration.

The timber industry was in a recession in the early eighties. Going home to join the family company or finding a job in engineering was not in the cards. I was hired as a project manager for a small, family-owned construction company in Spokane. We settled in to raise our family.

I hated it. Not because of the wonderful people I was working for, but because it was not home. I was living in a city. Our children were playing inside a chain link fence.

The last year we lived in Spokane, there were a couple of young, blonde girls snatched from yards and never found. PJ and I were fearful that our children were in danger. We had children who liked people. Echo Jo, in particular, was little miss social butterfly. She happily greeted every person walking by on the sidewalk. And since she loathed clothing as a three-year-old, the greeting was often conducted while naked.

One night after another little girl was snatched, we stayed up all night and talked about what we wanted for ourselves and our children. We talked about the career path I was on and how that path would probably mean living in a city somewhere. We remain to this day perpetually pleased that hundreds of millions of Americans love the city life, but that night we made a decision to pull up stakes and return to Montana. We wanted to raise our children and finish our lives in the luxury of the rural environment where I had grown up.

Chapter 4: Finding My Way Back Home

In January of 1984, I drove to Montana to discuss our decision with the larger family. I proposed rejoining Vincent Logging as a worker and a helper on the business management side of the operations. Dad did not know at the time that I had overheard his and Mom's discussion following the Iowa Basics test almost twenty years earlier. But I knew of the internal struggle with me moving back and taking part in our heritage. We never discussed those internal struggles openly until years later. I just told Dad and Mom and my three brothers, who were all involved in the family business, that I longed to come home. I did not care if I had to, as my older brother Will put it, 'strap on a tin bill and pick shit with the chickens,' I just wanted to return and raise my children.

Vincent Logging was, at that time, having a tough go of it while trying to make it through the early 1980s timber recession brought on by a collapse of the new home market nationwide. Vincent Logging primarily did logging jobs only when road building for timber sales was not possible, such as in the dead of winter when the ground was too frozen or the snow too deep to economically build logging roads. I discussed with them what I had learned in college and how my background might help. We could broaden what Vincent Logging was involved in as a way to broaden our economic base and possibly save the company. We reviewed the potential of becoming a primary bidder for national forest timber sales.

For nearly two decades, Vincent Logging had subcontracted logging road construction and logging for the large private industrial land and sawmill owners in the area. The timber companies owned some of their own land and contracted with the United States Forest Service (USFS) and Montana to manage some of those public lands. The timber companies no longer maintained their own work force in the woods but, rather, had dozens of subcontractors like Vincent Logging who completed the task of building roads to access timber, harvest, ship the logs to their plants and complete all necessary restoration and reforestation. Vincent Logging ended up doing a lot of the USFS work because Dad and my brothers did a good job for the companies and seemed to be able to 'get along' with the federal and state land-managing professionals.

It became clear to me that a better route for Vincent Logging was to become a prime or primary contractor rather than working as a subcontractor. With over 80 percent of the timber base in northwest Montana owned by the USFS and the state of Montana, there were enough timber management and road-building contracts available to allow us to successfully and competitively bid on and secure needed work. The potential profit margins would be greater if we secured contracts for completing the logging road construction, harvesting and restoration required of a prime contractor working on public lands.

To act as a prime contractor, there were additional financial, bonding, insurance and reporting needs that must be met. I suggested my business background might help in that regard. I hoped that if we were no longer under the thumb of the large companies, and had more control of our costs and income, we might be able to right the ship that was listing precariously.

To our great joy, the family welcomed us back with open arms. In February of 1984, I started the process of moving my family home. For the first month, I drove back and forth from Spokane as PJ worked to close down her daycare. I worked with Mom to get up to speed on the business operations and began to get our financial situation in position to secure the needed bonding to act as a prime contractor for the state and federal governments. I also worked in the woods with the crews, doing anything I could to help.

We had no place to live, so we purchased a new 'double-wide' mobile home and prepared a location to set the home on the land I grew up on. Only a few hundred feet from Dad and Mom's house, it wasn't where we wanted to be, exactly, but it was where we could afford to be for the time. And it turned out wonderful. Our plan was to live in that location for a few years and then build a home.

The mobile home was delivered during the last week of February, 1984. Fortunately, we had a very light winter that year so the ground was thawed enough to lay the concrete foundation necessary to set the mobile home. Dad and my brothers assisted in digging water lines and laying the electrical lines to our house. By the time the mobile home arrived, we were ready.

PJ and I tied up the loose ends of our lives in Spokane and moved for good the last week of February. The thrill of driving down the driveway of the place I was raised and once again being able to call it 'home' was incredible. I had been gone for eleven long years. I wanted to return for eleven long years. And now, at long last, I was going to be able to offer to my children the magic and wonder of living in the forest and among the mountains and wildlife I loved.

This time of year for loggers and road builders in the northwest of Montana is busy, but not in an income generating way. It is the time of year when the snow, having reached its maximum depths, begins to melt. As the sun begins its ascent into the middle of the sky, it warms the ground and begins to thaw the frost that can reach over to over four feet deep in the forest areas. The roads become too soft to haul heavy loads and begin to 'break up' if heavy trucks operate on them. This is why the spring months in cold logging country are called 'spring breakup.' During 'break up,' no wood can be shipped to sawmills and all of the heavy equipment needs to be moved to locations where repairs and maintenance can be completed for the upcoming logging season. Vincent Logging's machinery was moved to the shop on our land and the crew descended on each piece with a 'to do' list, wrenches, parts and paint. Dad and my brothers were the mechanical wizards who kept the machinery maintained on a tight budget. I ordered parts, handed tools to the wizards and marveled at their ingenuity and expertise.

During the first year we moved back, I moved the 'office' of the company out of Dad and Mom's house and into our large master bedroom. It was cozy, but it worked. I would work on equipment or on the job during the day, and work the books at night. Mom and PJ assisted with bookkeeping and answering the phone. I use the term 'assisted' loosely. I had a sign on my desk that asked, 'Do you want to talk to the man in charge or the woman who knows what is going on?' We made for a pretty good team, and soon had the books and financial records in shape to secure bonding and begin bidding on timber sales as a prime contractor.

In the late spring, I started the process of bidding on timber sales and road building projects for the USFS. We continued to secure negotiated subcontracting jobs for building the roads and harvesting the timber for the private timber companies, but our focus was getting out on our own. By the end of that first summer, we had secured some nice projects as prime contractors and our financial situation improved dramatically.

Our office needs required more room, so we built an office addition onto our mobile home. Mom, PJ and I each had an office space and we had a conference area for regularly scheduled family business meetings. The family members were given a monthly salary with bonus options based upon profitability, and each member and their families were covered with health, life and disability insurance. At the end of 1984, we were among the first loggers in the area to completely computerize our office operations. Though they now seem like dinosaurs, our first IBM AT desktop computer revolutionized the way we tracked and analyzed input costs and income streams.

With business looking up, we added some new and new-to-us machinery to our line-up and developed two road building crews with dozers and excavators, and two logging crews with log skidders, mechanical harvesters and processors, log loaders and the required fire-fighting equipment that was needed on summer logging jobs. We also purchased a logging truck to haul both logs and equipment from job to job.

Just as it is with all natural resource machinery, whether in farming, mining or energy development, the machinery itself is not cheap. It is absurdly easy to spend a million dollars, even if you buy used, so we needed to keep our equipment operating to pay off the loans secured at our bank. Our bank was our life line from operating season to operating season. Each spring, as the needs of the equipment were presented to me on lists of 'must do,' 'ought to do' and 'want to do,' I would work up a maintenance and repair plan with the family and go visit the place with the money – the bank. Our banking needs were, for decades, discussed with and met by our family banker, John Johanson and First National Bank and Glacier Bank in Libby. Without their assistance each year, we would not have survived very long.

My role with Vincent Logging was varied. I offered business management, did the bidding on our jobs, helped Mom and PJ keep the books up on the company (payroll, billing, etc) and worked in the field as a sawyer during the day when and where I could. It was heaven. In June of 1986, we added the fourth and final child to our family – our youngest son, Vance. We had a full house. Full of kids, full of love and full of joy and happiness.

The payroll swelled during the mid and late 1980s and we soon had 65 families working under our wing. We had two logging sides operating most of the time along with two road-building or land development sides. Our fleet of equipment grew to include road building dozers, rock blasting equipment, excavators, log harvesting and processing machines, log skidding and loading machinery along with log hauling trucks, lowboys to haul machinery from job to job and a fleet of crewcabs (or crummies in logger lingo) to get our crews to their respective jobs. Much of the log hauling for our operations was done through subcontractors who owned one or many trucks. They could respond to our fluctuating needs as we moved logs from the forest to the dozens of sawmills to which we marketed. Since these subcontractors moved our product to market, we relied heavily on them and were fortunate to have a number of outstanding log hauling partners.

As the company grew and began to prosper, the children were thriving with piles of cousins within arm's reach, tons of family and friends to assist in co-parenting and they were doing well in school. Schools were, in fact, one of the driving forces behind our decision to come home. Montana has outstanding public schools. In national rankings, the state as a whole has long been fighting it out for top of the heap in all facets of standardized testing.

I knew from my own childhood experience that the schooling my kids would get would set them up well for higher education and life. A classic example of how the schools stack up was when we moved in 1984. Chas was in an advanced class in Spokane where he, as a first grader, shared a classroom with second grade students. We thought he would make the move smoothly to the Montana schools, but were shocked when the teachers at our rural school (McGrade Elementary) had to go into the kindergarten room to find the scholastic materials Chas had been using in the 'advanced class' in Spokane. Thankfully, the teachers were of the same excellent stock I had enjoyed as a child, and they tutored him through the remainder of the first grade. He was caught up by the start of second grade.

The hours were long, the work was hard and the risk of being in a small family business was trying at times. But we believed that Vincent Logging was the foundation that would secure a long term future for all of us involved. That foundation, however, would soon be shaken.

Chapter 5: The End of Vincent Logging

The early years of Vincent Logging were much like the early years of thousands of family-owned, natural resource businesses, be they farms, ranches, fishing boats or small mines. In an effort to keep the machinery rolling, weekends were often spent on family 'outings' that somehow or other revolved around equipment maintenance. Dad, Mom, their four boys and any friends silly enough to stay the weekend got the opportunity to slap on a pair of overalls and hand Dad wrenches while he performed maintenance or repairs to the machines that generated the money needed to keep our family afloat. We needed to have the machinery operating by the time Dad returned to the 'brush' with the crew early Monday morning.

During the week, while us kids went to school, Mom assumed her position in the family home's office. As we boys got older, our job opportunities with the family business changed. Some of my first 'real' work in the woods included wintertime shoveling to remove snow from the base of trees so sawyers could cut them close to the frozen ground. I also got to do the fun work of 'picking sticks,' a process where we did final clean-up of debris embedded in newly built road surfaces.

The Kootenai National Forest, where we live, grows over 400 million board feet of new timber per year. Today, the forest mortality, due to insect infestations, disease, wind throw, root rot and fire, is approaching that same total. Thirty years ago we were removing just over 200 million board feet per year. This was enough wood fiber for five sawmills (some big, some small). It was also enough to keep many logging outfits busy, including the 65 employees working for Vincent Logging.

During the mid-1980s, there were growing indications that forest management was going to be under attack. There was an increasingly vocal group adhering to the school of thought that nature should be sole manager of our forests. While the writing was on the walls, few in our industry gave much credence to the claims being made about overharvesting or supposed decimation of the public's treasured forests. We knew the claims were false. We knew we plant six trees for every tree we harvest. We also knew we were doing our best to do a better job every day. It was, coincidentally, our efforts to do a better job that yielded my first clue to the nature of the folks we would be dealing with across the next several decades.

The logger members of the Montana Logging Association were concerned that there was a growing call for passage of a state-based regulatory regime similar to what other states in the west have – a forest practices act. It was our belief that such an act, written by legislators and not foresters, would not be in the best interest of forest managers or even in the best interests of the forest landscapes. We decided to get in front of the issue and begin to write our own compliance measures for issues important to us and the public. The first issue we tackled was management of forests in or around the water of streams, marshes and lakes. The sensitive riparian areas of our ecosystems need special treatment if we are to protect the water quality and quantity in our waterways. Most loggers love to fish, too, and were learning we could limit our impacts on our treasured water resources if we changed the way we operated.

Bud Clinch was our safety manager for the association and

Keith Olson, the association's executive director, put him in the lead to develop a Best Management Practices regime to answer the challenge we faced concerning forest management in riparian areas. His work was stellar. He gathered the appropriate brain trust around him and the committee crafted the framework that would define how we operate in or around waterways.

Their conclusions were compiled into a booklet that served as the centerpiece for rethinking our ground operations near water and the association began holding training sessions with loggers to teach them the new, self-imposed rules. That we were leading the charge was a source of great pride for the logging community. We were able to look at the public, elected leaders and governmental institutions and tell them we understood their concerns, we were being proactive to address those concerns and that we fully intended to be part of the solution to the problems both they and we had identified.

As a result, we completely changed how we operated when we were in a watershed. We also set up an independent 'committee' of foresters, conservationists, government agency employees and academics that would complete random 'audits' on our activities and give us a yearly 'report card.' The report card would let us know how we were doing collectively and by individual logger and project. It highlighted what needed further work. The first few audit years revealed nearly 90 percent compliance with the newly formed rules, but our goal was to hit 100 percent compliance. The training intensified with each season and within a few short years we were near 100 percent.

Nonetheless, we were baffled that we remained on the front page of the newspapers in the state. Groups continued making claims that Montana loggers were destroying our waters. Week after week, the headlines misinformed the people of Montana and ignored the reality of what our third-party audits were revealing. In frustration, the Montana Logging Association asked the leader of one of the groups making the claims to attend our annual meeting and explain to our members their concerns.

Michael Scott, then president of the Montana Wilderness Society, accepted our invitation and attended our annual meeting in Bozeman. He was courteous enough to answer questions after he presented his argument against logging, and he gave one answer that was pretty revealing about the nature of the conflict that was brewing. Mr. Scott was asked to give a percentage that indicated his group's perception of water quality problems in our state being caused by logging. "Three percent," he said

He was then asked what percentage of that three percent was caused by current practices and not legacy practices of past forest management. He said that he thought about twenty percent of the three percent was caused by current practices. In other words, according to the Montana Wilderness Society, current Montana logging practices were responsible for 0.6 percent of the water quality problems in our state. Why, then, was his group consistently denigrating our industry for our practices if they felt that 99.4 percent of the problems with water lay elsewhere? His answer, given with a bit of a chuckle, was: 'You are visible, and you are easy.'

I was incensed, naturally. Their fundraising strategy was to fight an industrial practice they readily admitted was only a minute overall part of an overall concern. We were being attacked in the media because we were an 'easy' target and they could raise money without a public backlash.

I was also concerned. Their strategy had every chance at working, and working well. Our industry is very visible, especially in the Rocky Mountains. Our workplaces are rarely in flat places where it is hard to see. They are scattered across the faces of the hillsides and can be seen from every highway, freeway and back road in the state. When we enter a forested area to do our management, we enter an area that is either stocked or overstocked with trees; beautiful, lovely trees. And when we are done, the tree part is missing and all that is left is a stump; an ugly stump. We *are* visible. I was also concerned because he may have been right about loggers being 'easy.' His implication was that we could be beaten up and really no one but us would care. We are not exactly the segment of society most revered by the public at large. We whack down trees.

What his comment did for the loggers of Montana was to

reconfirm our need and our desire to professionalize our operations through increased training and to continue to improve our operations. We didn't want to be an easy target. We decided to double down on our outreach to the people of the state and communicate with them about who we are and what we are doing for their forests and their streams. Our effort at leading this discussion has, to this day, enabled us to avoid having a regulatory regime (such as a forest practices act) imposed on us by those unfamiliar with the realities our forests.

During this same time period, the abuse of the United States Forest Service (USFS) appeals process by those who wished to halt logging was just beginning. A forest management 'appeal' is a public-engagement process wherein citizens can file an objection to a forest management decision. The objection must be successfully responded to by the agency before the management can proceed. Anti-forest management individuals and groups were successfully paralyzing the managing agency with massive quantities of appeals. As such, there were less and less timber sales available for Vincent Logging and other contractors to bid on. The area's sawmills were no longer able to control the amount of logs coming into their mills through price adjustments. They were concerned about securing their required share of raw logs coming off of federal lands, so they began to bid directly on USFS timber sales. The small loggers that had historically bid for the right to complete the management plans were now easily outbid by the larger entities that did the wood processing. Vincent Logging and dozens of other loggers in our area who had worked to become prime contractors were once more forced to become subcontractors to the sawmills and timber companies. The profit margins at Vincent Logging, and other outfits like it, shrank considerably.

Loggers in Montana were not alone. The logging industry throughout the west was beginning to collapse. Our business profits contracted even further when the spotted owl situation on the far west coast area closed down hundreds of sawmills, thereby putting many loggers out of work. Communities reliant upon public land management were collapsing. Many of the loggers from the coast found their way inland in an effort to survive, thus saturating the marketplace and driving the prices we could get from logging below the breakeven point.

In the early 1990s, Vincent Logging sent logging crews as far away as Havre and Livingston, Montana, in an effort to find work that paid enough to breakeven. Our crews stayed in motels and camper trailers and were up to 400 miles from their families. It was tough living that was hard on our workers and our families. It was also hard to make a profit and, for several years, we did not. We downsized our operations, sold some equipment (prices tanked along with the rest of the industry so we took a beating on most of it), laid off the vast majority of our crews and operated with as much family as we could in order to make ends meet.

In 1992, we were forced to reorganize under bankruptcy protection. It was a painful process and it took seven long years to repay our debtors, but we did. We also had hope that the situation in and around Libby would stabilize, America would understand a healthy forest required some harvesting to manage an overstocked landscape and we would be able to re-engage our workers and bring our crews home. Sadly, this did not come to pass.

The family was going through its own issues during this time period, and much of it was brought on by the stress of trying to survive. My older brother, Will, left the company in the mid-1990's and started an excavation company in hopes that he could make it without being on the road. In 1995, Mom had a recurrence of an earlier bout with cancer and passed away in January of 1996. Losing Mom was a shock from which the family business never really recovered. Dad worked his way through his grief but no amount of work can cover the pain of losing your life's mate at the time when you are supposed to be winding down and reap some reward for a life well-lived with your partner.

My younger brother, Steve, was diagnosed with multiple sclerosis (MS) during this same time period. We knew something was wrong with him. He was operating a mechanized processor and was having quality control issues with log lengths and diameters. Those issues are critical when processing logs for use in the mills, and he took our brotherly ribbing about any mistakes without much fanfare. He finally, begrudgingly, one day admitted he could not see very well, his hands were numb, his legs were going numb and he thought something might be wrong. Typical tough-it-out logger reaction to a failing body. We were horrified, and scared. Thankfully, it was MS and not something worse, and though he had to stop logging while he got this new medical challenge under control, he was alive and could live a full life. With treatment he has been able to rejoin the workforce and is now operating a log-sorting machine for a nearby sawmill.

With the family business and family members struggling, our oldest son, Chas, left school in Oregon and returned home to log for a year. He joined my younger brother Scott, Dad and a small crew and tried to find a way to salvage what was left of the company. They went wherever they could find work, but with every contractor in every area of the west facing the same dilemma as Vincent Logging, the pickings were slim. Finally, in 2004, we had a family meeting and folded up the tent. It was among the toughest things I have ever done.

By then I was just doing the books for the company and I was making my living speaking and doing consulting work in the company started with my business partner, Tammy Johnson. The money earned from those efforts paid off the final hundreds of thousands of dollars of remaining debt. PJ and I purchased the last few pieces of equipment from the shell of Vincent Logging. They now sit in our yard, and may one day be the foundation for Chas or another family member to pick up the Vincent Logging flag and try to fly it once more. Hope is eternal.

Chapter 6: The Town with a Heart

As Vincent Logging struggled to survive, so too, did our town.

Prior to the collapse of the timber sale program, the economy in Libby was cyclical, because of commodity prices, but it was nonetheless robust and resilient. The blue-collar town enjoyed middle-income family wage jobs and most of the jobs included benefit packages that provided them and their families with access to medical care.

In the 1960s through the 1980s, the national forest surrounding Libby provided over 200 million board feet per year for local processing. By the end of the 1990s, the harvest off of the Kootenai had shrunk to less than 40 million board feet. The local loggers like Vincent Logging were forced to lay off massive numbers of employees and as a result the local sawmills were forced to curtail their production. The Louisiana Pacific Mill in Libby, which had employed over 100 men and women, closed in the late 1990s. The family owned sawmill and stud mill in Libby, which had been operating for a century and at one time employed over 1,000 in the milling complex alone, closed in the late 1990s. The plywood plant's 200 plus employees were able to keep their jobs until that plant was shuttered in 2003.

This downturn in timber was compounded by the necessary closing of the WR Grace (300 plus direct jobs) asbestos-laden vermiculite mine and the closing of Asarco's 300-employee Troy mine because of depressed silver and copper prices. The Noranda Mining Company's proposed mining project up Libby Creek employed some 75 families in the early 1990s, but was closed down when regulatory excess made the project untenable for the Canadian Mining company and they moved their crews to Peru.

The impact of losing over 2,500 direct, family-wage resource industry jobs in less than a decade were felt everywhere in town. Main street businesses folded. Our area closed three grade schools, melded what was left of the elementary school into the middle school, shifted one more grade into the high school building and laid off a sizeable number of teachers. Further, the local hospital, once largely supported by the sawmill and mine's union employees with benefits, was left to figure out how to survive when faced with an aging population, fewer jobs with fewer health benefits and an increasing reliance upon Medicare and Medicaid payments.

When the natural resource jobs first started to leave in the 1990s, many of the families thought that there would surely be a resurgence. The jobs would be back soon, they figured ("good heavens, we have lots of trees, surely we'll start logging again when the public understands that if we don't log they'll just burn"). As a result, many of the 'dads' took what they thought were temporary jobs in Alaska or Nevada, operating equipment and coming home when they could with a check for their family. This left many moms as single mothers and kids in disjointed families. When the jobs did not return to the area, and when the families lived like this for several years, family disintegration ran rampant through our community. Further, many moms needed to take a local, often minimum wage job to help make ends meet.

Studies have shown that increases in unemployment lead to

a corresponding rise in social ills such as child abuse, sex abuse, alcohol abuse, suicides and drug abuse. We, in Libby, are statistically valid. The family crisis in our forest community produced spikes in young adults with issues in drug and alcohol abuse, unplanned pregnancies… the list goes on.

As the economic underpinnings of Libby began to unravel, so too did the health insurance safety nets for the families of the area. Lost jobs means lost benefits for the employee and the employee's family. For many in our blue-collar town, this was the first time in their lives they had been without insurance, and the consequences were quick in the coming. One uninsured young lady in her mid-twenties, Sally Sauer, became the focus of the community when she contracted a virus that attacked her heart. The virus was deadly, and it was soon clear the only thing that could keep Sally from passing away was a heart transplant. The medical facility was in Spokane, only 3 ½ hours away, but the cost of the procedure for the uninsured was over $100,000. Sally was in trouble.

Sally's father, a longtime forester for one of the area's sawmills, was well known and word soon passed through the town that Sally and her family needed help. When you are isolated, you must be fairly self-dependent. At the same time, when a community is isolated, the first look for help when help is needed is inside of the community itself. Some loggers got together and decided that two things needed to happen if Sally was to survive: we needed to get our federal delegation to assist her family in getting her onto Medicaid to help with the costs, and we needed to raise the needed money in case the Medicaid assistance took too long to cover the heart transplant.

And so, a plan to get Sally her life-saving heart was put in motion. We loggers approached the private timber land and sawmill owners to ask if they had a section of timber (one square mile) that was ready for harvesting immediately. The plan was to have loggers do the management and harvest the logs with donated equipment and volunteers. Local log truck owners would donate their trucks and time to haul the logs to the local sawmill for processing. Local mill workers would volunteer their time to process the logs into boards and plywood. The proceeds from selling the material would be donated to a fund to cover the costs of Sally's heart transplant. The timber company (Champion International), the log haulers and the mill workers agreed to the plan and while Sally was barely hanging on in a Spokane hospital, the town of Libby went to work.

Local school children made large red cloth hearts to place on the front of the logging trucks hauling Sally's logs, and the local weigh station weigh master agreed to look the other way as the trucks passed his normally required inspection site on US Highway 2, and roared towards the waiting processing crews at the sawmill and plywood plant. The local 50-watt radio station, KLCB, kept the town apprised of both the action in the woods and the sawmill and the slowly deteriorating condition of Sally in her hospital room 165 miles away. Community members, including retired people, retailers, kids in our schools, everyone in town, kicked in what cash they could to help reach the goal of $100,000. A separate committee led by my close friend and the owner of the local Hallmark Store, Connie Wood, burned up the phone lines to our US Representatives and Senators, begging them to assist in pushing through the needed Medicaid coverage just in case we didn't reach our targeted monetary amount in time. Montana's Senator Conrad Burns assigned a person to the task, and the wheels of the federal government began to slowly turn.

The doctors in Spokane heard about what the town was doing and offered their services even if the money had not been secured yet. They too were determined to do their part and join the small town's push to save Sally.

Finally, with all of the needed financial security and medical expertise in place, we just needed a heart. We knew that a heart for Sally was going to be gained through a tragedy visited upon another family somewhere in the inland northwest, and that weighed on us, but we also hoped that such a tragedy may be a bit easier to endure for a family if they knew their loved one had given life to someone else's loved one. We waited. Sally waited, and her struggling heart was slowly giving out on her. For days the family phoned in to the radio station with status reports to let the town know how Sally was doing and if there was any news on a match for her transplant. As the hours and days passed, it began to look as if the virus was going to win and the town prayed for Sally, the family and for acceptance of God's will – whatever that may be.

When it looked as if all hope was lost, and it looked as if Sally had no more than a day to live, the miracle happened and was blasted over KLCB and shouted throughout the town. A MATCH HAD BEEN FOUND! Sally was being taken off of the machines and wheeled into surgery. She was very, very weak and the doctors told the family that the procedure was going to be difficult and risky, but that they would do everything in their power to bring her back to them alive.

To say that the entire community was on edge would be an understatement. It was as if the town itself was holding its breath. With no internet at the time, radio and telephone were the only ways to transfer information and everyone hovered over their radios and sat by their phones waiting for word from the Sauer family in Spokane. Heart transplant procedures take a long time, and as the hours went by, and the 'no news' reports were shared over the radio, the tension built. Periodic reports from the doctors were shared by the family, and we all knew that the doctors and Sally were fighting a good fight but the outcome was clearly in doubt.

When the news from the operating room to the Cardiac Care Unit was that of 'success,' and that her new heart was beating like crazy, the town went nuts. In living rooms and businesses, townspeople shouted out in relief and greeted each other with high fives, hugs, tears and sobs of joy.

When Sally was finally able to come home, she was greeted by a community that needed her as much as she needed them. We couldn't fix our economic woes but we damn well did what was needed to help fix Sally. Two years after her transplant, Sally participated in the national transplant games in Atlanta and brought home two bronze medals.

Senator Burns and the local committee had also expedited

the coverage of most of the medical costs, and the remaining money, over $100,000, was moved into a hastily formed (and still surviving) Sally Sauer Community Medical Fund. I am proud to have served on the fund's board. The fund cares for local people whose medical bills threaten to swamp them.

Soon after Sally's issue was resolved, we learned that a truck driver who hauled logs for local contractors (including Vincent Logging) had received news that his five-year-old daughter had a congenital heart defect that needed fixing, or she would not see adulthood. His family, like all logging families at that time, was struggling to survive and also had no medical coverage. We had the Sally Sauer Community Medical Fund set up by then and we could front the needed capital, but had determined that when money was used from the Fund we needed to replace it.

A new cause swept through town, and the small but big-smiling, front-tooth-missing Amanda Johnson became the new 'we can do this' community focus. I did some rough calculations and determined that, even with the number of people who were laid off and unemployed, if the entire town worked one hour and donated the hours' worth of wages to the Medical Fund, we could pay the $60,000 estimated costs of Amanda's heart surgery. I called local businesses and asked if they would pass word along. The businesses not only said 'yes' but 'hell yes' and many offered to match what their employees contributed. Connie Wood set up a war room in the back of the Hallmark store and we were off and running again.

At one in the afternoon on February the 19th, the fire siren at the volunteer fire house blasted, all of the church bells in town tolled, Amanda was hauled down the main street of town on the back of a fire truck and 'Hour Amanda' became a reality. Libby native and Montana Governor Marc Racicot came home to officiate a benefit basketball game between the Libby Loggers and the Troy Trojans and thousands more dollars were raised. Again, we met our monetary goal and, more importantly, Amanda received her heart surgery and entered the first grade as a typical, fun-loving, energetic six-year-old.

We still weren't done. The following year a group of high

school students came to my office attached to the house. They had just learned that Kyle Rosling was in much the same trouble as Sally and Amanda. The senior Homecoming King had learned, while taking his medical examination for fall wrestling, that he had a heart issue threatening not only his participation in sports but his life. His father was a sawyer in the woods and, like so many others, was only able to find spotty employment and had no health insurance.

"You've done this before and now we need to do it for Kyle. Just tell us what to do," they said. 'Kids for Kyle' was launched that afternoon, and they embarked on a fundraising program that included auctioning off high school students for work around town, door to door campaigns and more. Money was raised, Kyle received his needed heart work, and is now the father of four wonderful kids of his own.

The hardest part of these efforts was not the organized giving. That was easy for the townspeople to do. It was welcomed and, in many ways, was needed as it served as self-healing for a town that was being economically devastated. We were able to turn inward and do something constructive to help ourselves.

The hardest part was the burden of receiving the 'gifts of giving' that each of the recipients and their families were saddled with. In order to get the town engaged, they had to be willing to offer themselves as the target for the generosity and kindness of their neighbors. Charity is not easily received by those who believe that you earn your way in life. I spent many hours working with the families as they tried to get their head around 'receiving.' The arguments that I made over and over, and the ones that I think helped the most, were that the town needed to do this as much for itself as for them, and that each of us knows that 'there but for the grace of God go I.' Any one of us could be next in their seat.

The principles and values of looking out for your neighbor, and treating others as you wish to be treated, are still alive in most rural communities. This is the culture that called me back so that I could raise my family after college. This is also the community fabric that is ripping when we undermine the economic stability of rural America. I often hear talking heads on television say we need to rediscover these values, so we can heal and bind our nation. Yet it would seem that we are our own worst enemy, and the only people stopping us from getting there is us.

Chapter 7: Rural America Today

How we manage our natural resources, whether through agriculture, mining, forestry, caretaking for animals (both wild and domesticated), and harvesting energy from water and wind, has long been the subject of great debate. What is, and is not, an acceptable use of our natural resources? Much of this comes down to who owns, or has rights, to such resources. But it's not just how we understand property rights, it's the rules, both governmental and social in nature, developed to enforce them.

It seems simple at first. You own the land, and it's yours, right? Yet assets and resources as valuable as land, minerals, air and other life-supporting necessities complicate things quickly. Even if you have the property rights, rules can give rise to the authorization of use, or rights to use, or even how you can use, certain properties. These are generally what we find in place when we want to exercise a right, such as fishing or collecting minerals or water – but many of these rules were not in place just a few short decades ago.

During my early years I became, along with the rest of the country, aware of the environmental impacts of American industrialization. I was just a young pup when I watched in horror as the square screen of our single-channel black and white television showed in real-time the combustion of the Cuyahoga River as it burned through Cleveland, Ohio. I got to see, on that same screen, fish swimming upside down in Lake Erie and knew that the Great Lakes were in trouble. I had never been to Los Angeles but I could see on television that their air was quickly becoming poisoned. I also got to witness the first view of our planet Earth from a distance as the Apollo astronauts beamed back to the ground-bound inhabitants their television stream showing our little blue ball bobbing along in blackness. It was clear that we had only one planet to call home, we were not going to get another planet to live on, and some of the things we were doing needed to change. As president of our middle school, I helped to organize the clean-up of the creek going by our school during the first Earth Day.

These sentiments, feelings of morality or ethical obligation, complicate how we use our natural resources. An individual may feel that something isn't 'right' and that may, for better or for worse, trump, in their mind, property rights. They may feel compelled to act in order to protect their 'interest' – the environment – and influence how we are managing nature's resources. We dig into this later as we look at the progression of the environmental movement.

My family did not own the forests of Montana. Much of this was owned by the United States Forest Service (USFS) or others who contracted out with us. Yet we lost our 'right' to log the forests as the owners of this land (public and private) were subject to externally applied rules as to how they could, or could not, exercise their property rights or manage the resource for the public's benefit. As such, we lost our business and our livelihood and our very way of life. At the same time, the public is losing the institutional knowledge necessary to manage resources and protect their environment.

My Dad, and those like him have, by the simple act of 'doing,' assembled more environmental knowledge about their forests, soils and the animals with whom they co-exist than they could have gotten from a pile of degrees from the world's most celebrated institutions. Their knowledge has come through the work of their hands. The bank of knowledge learned through the practical application of scientific theory is incredibly valuable, and often overlooked by those who are separated from the processes of natural resource management.

The divide between rural and urban settings has long been recognized. There have been significant investments in the areas of sociology, economics, geography and childhood studies to examine how views of urban versus rural locations impact perceptions, including perceptions of one's self.

My own story of self, as a young boy, highlights the many layers of this. Take, for instance, the Iowa Basics. There were my parents and their roles in society, and then there were the views of a seemingly well-meaning teacher, who changed my perception of my father through perhaps well-intentioned but ill-implemented actions to 'help' a pupil. We were rural, and my father's profession was decidedly rural. Researchers have long examined how a person's vision of their place in life (literally, in the case of rural versus urban geography) and chosen profession frame their own views of their worth.

Research, and common sense, has found that young people's narratives of identity often reflect the public narratives which construct hierarchies of places.[1] There is, arguably, a predisposition to label urban locales as potentially superior to rural ones. Could one's view of their own living situation color their views of other's living situations, chosen professions, and even taint how one expects others from varying locales to conduct themselves? Yes, it can. And not without unintended consequences when professions dealing with resource management are colored 'not worthy.'

The denigration of career choices involving resource management will not come without a cost to the environment. Destructive social stigmas often assist in making the leading

---

[1] Vanderbeck and Dunkley, 2003; page 242

—

export of our rural resource families and communities our well-educated, well-rounded youth. When the earth is home to the predicted 9 to 11 billion souls who all want food, clothing and shelter, it is going to take some pretty intelligent kids doing some pretty creative things to provide for those needs while protecting the planet. We need to have the assurance that the smart kids who desire to return to the fold of the largely rural resource management cultures are able to do so, and take their place in the long line of those proud of their heritage of stewardship and conservation.

To gain assurance that the next generation to engage in resource management can do so without a social class head trip, we must first be aware of social stigmas. Rural industries have often long downplayed the usual markers of professionalism that others in more urban settings expect. Several very obvious reasons contribute: soil is real (and necessary) and exists in greater quantities in many rural settings, dress codes vary necessarily (to avoid freezing in winter or for personal safety, for example) and lifestyles vary (45 minutes to the supermarket really changes your dinner plans). Further, several traditional markers of rural livelihoods, including the incorporation of children into activities on the farm, inconsistent and often extreme work hours and extreme outdoor work conditions, necessitate different behaviors than might not otherwise be seen as desirable by those not directly engaged in similar work or living situations. These are all beyond the control of anyone working in a rural profession.

Yet have we ever overplayed our uniqueness to such a degree that it impacts the views of our rural professions by those less likely to witness such lifestyles firsthand? Perhaps we ought to ask ourselves those tough questions. Popular media and television portray many of us in rural livelihoods in extreme filth or conducting grotesque aspects of our jobs. We are often portrayed as decidedly unprofessional. Think *Duck Dynasty*, or *Dirty Jobs*. When unprofessional behaviors become primetime television viewing fodder or, worse, are worn as a badge and proudly displayed to others, many of whom feel compelled to remain in the popularly accepted 'professional world' for whatever reason (social norms, social expectations, lack of first-hand exposure to any alternative, by choice), then we certainly aren't helping ourselves out any in the fight to be seen and treated as equals.

Oddly enough, a frequent misconception is that these roles *don't* require our applicators to spend some time at schools of higher learning. Modern resource management, be it farming, ranching, mining, fishing or logging, often requires years of academic pursuit beyond high school. I am a big believer and supporter of higher learning. I have completed and my children have completed their college degrees. Each of my kids fully understands, though, that all of the theory that is taught in our universities is just that – theory – and theory floats around in nah-nah land until some real person tries to apply that theory to the real ground with their real hands.

If one of my children or grandchildren decides that they would like to be a logger, or a farmer, or a rancher, or a fisherman, or work in the mining or energy fields, they will proudly do so. And without a social class head trip. Yet they will also do so with a degree of professionalism that will not necessarily come solely from a college education, to be clear.

If we act with a higher degree of professionalism, will society change the way they feel about our roles and the environment? We can certainly hope so, but we must also recognize that many of our beliefs about the way 'things are' are dependent upon social stigmas or expectations. Along with a generational recognition of the environmental impacts of man, I was far from alone in the early indoctrination of the mantra of 'nature is good, man is bad.' I saw *Bambi*, where evil man tried to kill the poor wildlife. I watched Disney movies where the animals were humanized and had to fight the wicked ways of humans in order to survive. This confused me, as it must have confused a lot of my generation, because where I grew up I thought man and nature co-existed. I thought man was a part of nature.

It is not too late to fix this problem. For example, the forests around where I live carry an enormous fuel load. To restore the health of our forest, we can recognize the longstanding, rich, symbiotic relationship between the forest and humankind. Our forests were under human management for some ten thousand years before being allowed to 'manage themselves.' When we understand how the hand of man has influenced our forest ecosystems, we can determine how to use management techniques that resurrect the eons-old methods of the Native Americans. We can selectively remove some of the trees and then conduct light, controlled burns to reintroduce the life-giving benefits of low, ground-hugging fires to our ecosystem. The management regime can be good for the forest, good for the species that rely on a healthy forest (including the grizzly bear) and, if done sustainably, good for the families and communities that live in the forest. Actually, forest health would benefit not just those who live in the forest, but also those who live near it, visit it, plan to visit it or even those who never plan to visit but simply sleep better at night knowing it exists.

For over twenty years, and throughout the west, stakeholder groups of concerned citizens have made many, many successive attempts to find common ground concerning management of our forest. We have been able to bring previously at-odds parties of interest to a common table of discussion and found that we all share one thing: a love of the forest. We have pounded out hard-fought conclusions concerning who, what, when, where and how we ought to be managing the forest for its health and the long-term sustainability of our forest communities.

We haven't made it all the way there yet. We have much, much more progress to make. My story thus far has been a personal one. It is the firsthand story of myself from a young boy living in the mountains of Montana on the tales of his pioneering grandparents to the man I am today. But the picture is much bigger, as we'll see. The problems confronting logging are few in light of the many others confronting various other natural-resource industries across the United States.

Part Two

From Sensitivity to Insanity

Chapter 8: The Start of a Movement

During my high school years, the Army Corps of Engineers built a very large dam, the Libby Dam, on the Kootenai River just north of Libby. Firsthand, I witnessed how man's actions can have a big and immediate impact on the natural environment. The dam was built for power generation and flood control, and it also provided a lot of temporary jobs for those in our area. The town expanded a great deal with the 2,400 men and women needed to build the dam.

While the electricity that is generated from the dam benefits humans, and the flood control is appreciated each spring in the towns that had for decades dealt with spring-time flooding, the dam is not without its negative impacts. The previously meandering portion of the Kootenai River was gone, and two small towns of Rexford and Warland that graced its banks were now at the bottom of a ninety-mile-long lake called Lake Koocanusa. 'Koo' is for Kootenai. 'Can' is for the miles of the reservoir that slop over into Canada. And 'usa' is for the USA.

During construction of the dam, the federal government informed the community they had another dam on the same river planned for later construction. They called it a 'reregulating' dam and it was to be placed a few miles downstream from the big Libby Dam. The intention of such a dam was to catch surplus water from the Kootenai River when Lake Koocanusa received heavy runoff and flows. This new dam would flood yet another stretch of the Kootenai River bottom and would also flood a section of the Fisher River drainage.

I knew that the new dam would once again provide for jobs for local people, but questioned whether or not the impacts to the local environment were worth it. Many local people pushed for the dam, but more than a few thought that 'One Dam Was Enough' and fought to keep it from being constructed. Additionally, just further downstream and east of Libby, are the beautiful Kootenai Falls. The Falls are a special place for locals, and were a special and sacred place for the Native Americans who lived here for eons. Shortly after the Libby Dam was built, a power company from northern Idaho discussed building a power generating facility in Kootenai Falls to take advantage of the powerfully surging waters. The Kootenai River would run through turbines at the foot of the falls and generate green power for consumers in the area. Again, while this idea had merit for providing power to consumers and would provide jobs for some folks in construction, I also questioned whether or not the impacts to the area were worth it.

After leaving high school and entering into junior college, I was honored to be elected the president of the student body at MT. Hood Community College. I used that platform to organize letter writing campaigns from the students in our school to encourage the federal government to change their minds on the reregulating dam and to disallow the construction of a power generating facility within Kootenai Falls. While we were not 'the' reason that both of these projects died on the drawing board, they gave me some insight into how regular people can interact with environmental decision-making in a constructive manner. Those who supported the projects did not see the interaction I participated in as constructive, but it did inform me about the power of citizen involvement.

I cite these examples because they served as my entre' into environmental activism. I was a logger's son and believed that while much of what man must do to survive involves necessary impacts to the environment, sometimes some things just go too far. I thought of myself as a conservationist and believed the actions I took to protect the environment that I loved were the right things to do. I thought I was a true member of the 'environmental movement.'

*   *   *

My own thoughts and feelings back in the late 60s and early 70s aligned with what was happening on the national stage. The pulse of the nation leading up to 1970 was a unique one. Involvement and engagement in political causes had become the social norm for swaths of the American population. There was very little political apathy amongst the youth. Campus activism ran rampant across the nation as students led the charge in protests against war. And there certainly wasn't any social media to detract from meaningful work towards change. Activism and engagement meant getting out on the streets, organizing and working hard. People knew that, they understood it and they leaned into it.

In addition to this, the importance of clean air and water, over the span of the preceding five to ten years, had leapt to the forefront of people's minds. As alluded to earlier, television sets were in nearly every living room. If you weren't living in the smog from traffic and factories, you were looking at it on your screen. And in 1969 the dual headline-grabbers of the massive Santa Barbara oil spill and the Cuyahoga River in Cleveland, which was burning (read: literally lit on fire), had set the stage. The image of the Cuyahoga River, with great spumes of smoke rising from its waters as it burned, was a picture that seared itself into people's minds. It is remembered to this day.

Change was on the horizon. Significant segments of the American population were experienced and prepared to organize and take action, given the anti-war movements and women's movement, amongst others. The environment was rising steadily as a source of concern. With the Cuyahoga River on fire and the Santa Barbara oil spill serving as catalysts, things were set in motion. While some action had been fomenting around the environment throughout the 1960s, a big page was about to turn for the environmental movement. An event was on the horizon that would launch the environment onto the front page of newspapers across the nation.

Then, on April 22nd, 1970, it happened. *The New York Times* ran a headline article, "Millions Join Earth Day Observances Across the Nation." It printed on the front page, above the fold, and underneath ran a black and white photo of thousands of people demonstrating peacefully in the street. It was the very first Earth Day in the history of the United States. Incredibly, it was also a spontaneous response at the grassroots level. No one body or organization was managing the 20 million demonstrators who participated, nor the thousands of schools and local communities who played a part in it as well. A tiny group of people had set things into motion, and the rest became history.

At the time, Secretary of the Interior Walter J. Hickel was quoted as saying, "I am optimistic about Earth Day and I hope it will not be the finale following one year of environmental awareness." Then President Nixon, although not participating directly, also expressed his hope that it would be more than a one-day event, but rather a new and sustained effort. Little did they know, at the time, that a flash-in-the-pan movement was not, whatsoever, a concern they needed to entertain.

It was not *The New York Times* alone who ran the story. On that very same day, many other newspapers across the country ran similar stories. *The Fort Collins Coloradoan* ran two front page articles, "Earth Day observance nationwide," alongside the far more practical, "Weather dampens Earth Day bicycling plans." *The Daily News* simply ran a full-page image with 'EARTH DAY!' Superimposed in bold, black letters. Yet perhaps most prescient, however, was the headline of *The Gaylord Nelson Newsletter* that ran several weeks later: "Earth Day – 1970 – Mass Movement Begins."

The headline did, in fact, turn out to be true. That very first Earth Day in 1970 is considered by many to be the birth of the modern environmental movement. While energy had been slowly growing leading up to that year, the environment still wasn't largely considered or discussed by large portions of society. And although Rachel Carson's bestseller Silent Spring, published eight years prior in 1962, had done much to set the stage for the inception of the movement, the environment still wasn't a trending topic in mainstream America.

One dedicated politician, and a dedicated team of volunteers, did much to change this. Gaylord Nelson, whose 1970 newsletter headline predicted the future of the environmental movement, was, at the time, a senator for Wisconsin. Nelson's interest in the environment was neither fleeting nor superficial. It was, in many ways, his calling. Born in 1916 in Clear Lake, Wisconsin, he became Wisconsin's governor in 1958 during which time he was known as the 'Conservation Governor.' He condensed Wisconsin's sprawling bureaucracy into a single Department of Resource Development, established a Youth Conservation Corps to create green jobs for over 1,000 unemployed young people and fought to earmark $50 million for the Outdoor Recreation Action Program. This program acquired land for conversion into public parks and wilderness areas. It was the extreme popularity of these conservation measures that catapulted him into the US Senate in 1962.

The idea for Earth Day started small. It was to be a "national teach-in on the environment." He and his office, alongside a few other key players across the country, were responsible for launching and coordinating the very first Earth Day. He persuaded Congressman Pete McCloskey, a conservation-minded Republican, to join him (a Democrat) as his co-chair. They recruited Denis Hayes from Harvard to be their national coordinator.

As the headlines of the day and history shows, the response from the American public far exceeded anyone's expectations or even imagination. The type of news coverage it garnered, and the sheer number of headlining stories that ran across the nation, marked a landslide success for what was, in truth, a grassroots movement lead mostly by volunteers, a staff of less than 100, a single professor and two politicians.

The period of time immediately prior and after the first Earth Day marked a rare political alignment across parties. Efforts to protect the environment garnered support from both Republicans and Democrats, as well as across demographics. Urban and rural alike were united in a common cause. This alliance across parties led to a powerful few years in legislative accomplishment.

There was a lot of momentum, a lot of sensitivity and awareness, and a lot of excitement and hope for the future prospects of the environmental movement. It was a movement with the best of intentions, kicked off at the grassroots level and supported politically by both sides of the aisle. Yet elements of this timely, necessary and growing social movement were destined to radically change.

Chapter 9: Brake Lines & Death Threats

My first interface with the dark and ugly side of the environmental movement came as a rude shock to my system, particularly given that I considered myself an 'environmentalist.' I love the environment. I do, and always did, believe humans have a responsibility to respect, care for and, where possible, nurture the natural systems that keep our planet alive. I firmly believe there are cases where humans can make mistakes in trying to 'subdue' the wild, and the public has a right to interface with decision-making when their environment is being impacted.

As such, I was a supporter in spirit of much of the social movement that rose from the concerns of the public during the 1960s. Yet when I started to believe that elements of the environmental movement were going too far, I spoke out.

Historically, there had been no seat at the table for the communities of people who needed both a healthy environment *and* a healthy economy. I resolved myself to trying to figure out how to give our 'impacted other' a seat at the table of debate and a voice in the deliberations. My voice was not always welcome, particularly by those who enjoyed the stark black and white nature of an 'us vs. them' debate that positioned them as sole guardians of a public interest they had total control over defining.

At first, the consequences of my speaking out were fairly innocuous. I began receiving letters and phone calls from unknown individuals who were extremely upset with my views. The calls, at first, were nothing more than irrational ramblings of persons who would not give their names but disagreed with my views. A few unsigned letters with vicious statements of disapproval were sent that echoed the sentiments of the phone callers. No threats were made. They were just statements of disagreement with requests to "shut up."

During the summer of 1989, however, the nature of the calls began to change. The dialogue of the perpetrators became more and more vicious. The disagreements and request to have me "shut up" began to be coupled with threats about "getting me" if I didn't. Then the threats realized.

While working on a job in the Kootenai National Forest, our companies' equipment was sabotaged. Someone poured dirt into the engine of one of our dozers. When the dozer engine failed, Dad was, thankfully, operating the dozer on flat ground. Since the hydraulics on this particular 100,000-pound machine are directly connected to the engine, and since the hydraulics make the brakes of this machine work, had the failure occurred on steep ground Dad would have been the jockey of an out-of-control, 50-ton deadly projectile.

Then the brake lines on one of our dump trucks were cut. The compromised brakes were discovered before anyone was injured and about the same time we learned the hydraulic lines on one of our excavators were cut. Since laborers worked under the excavator boom and the boom was controlled by its hydraulic system, we were fortunate the imminent failure of the boom was averted before anyone was physically injured. It was sheer luck that no one died. During this same time period, other local logging contractors had equipment sabotaged. Catching those sabotaging our machinery and thereby threatening the lives of those unsuspectingly working around our equipment was given shockingly little attention, especially when one considers the potential for impact, even if such potential was not personally realized.

The approach to the equipment sabotage was exactly as outlined in <u>Ecodefense: A Field Guide to Monkey Wrenching</u>. This book was published by one of the founders, Dave Foreman, of the radical environmental advocacy group Earth First!. However, the criminals at our job site did not leave a calling card. They slipped away. Yet two summers later, in the newsletter *Wild Rockies Review*, Earth First! ran a call-to-action in the inland northwest. In that advertisement for eco-terrorists, they included a drawing of a burning dozer situated on a map of northwestern Montana with the caption of 'Burn that Dozer.' Posted on campuses throughout the area, the advertisement's plea went to students looking for summer work and promised room and board for those wanting to spend the summer petrifying resource workers and managers.

Shortly after our equipment was sabotaged, the number of threatening phone calls and the viciousness of those calls escalated. I called the authorities and asked for help, but was told that unless I could prove that I had been harmed, there was nothing that could be done.

The threats were acted out on stage when a group of extremists in Missoula, Montana, developed a short skit in which I was portrayed as a hunter of animals along with then US Representative Ron Marlenee. At the end of the skit, as performed and videotaped on the steps of the federal building in Missoula, I was shot and killed to protect the animals. My family, and myself, became alarmed. Actually, not alarmed, more like terrified.

In the fall of 1989, the *CBS News* show "60 Minutes" called and asked if I would be available for an interview on eco-terrorism. Ed Bradley interviewed me in our workshop and on one of our logging jobs. The show aired in the spring of 1990. Shortly after the episode aired, the producer called, worried, to tell me that the *CBS* studio had received an inordinate number of phone calls from persons who were asking for the address of

Earth First!. The producer was concerned that by airing the show, *CBS* may have inadvertently focused unwanted attention on me and my family. The callers seemed to be happy to learn that there was an avenue for expressing the hatred that they felt. The producer's warning proved prophetic.

To my horror, the threatening phone calls turned from focusing on the harm to be done to myself to harm to my children. Callers threatened, in graphic detail, to perform sexual and physical torture on my children before killing them. I was told that I would be forced to watch. One caller played a recorded version of a song written about my children, another was a recording of children screaming in pain and terror for their mother to "help me, help me, help me."

Finally, my local sheriff installed phone traps on my phone line, but because of the antiquated system of phones in our area, the trapping was not effective if the call originated outside of our area code or our local phone company. No one was ever trapped or caught.

With the aid of Senator Conrad Burns' office, the FBI and state authorities were called in. Yet again, I was informed that until something happened there was little that they could do. It was suggested that I carry a concealed weapon and that I teach my wife and children how to handle and fire a gun. It was never made clear to me what type of investigation was attempted into those who threatened my family and me.

I was alerted on occasions when the authorities got wind of what they deemed a 'credible threat.' I was advised to "be careful" when giving speeches. On those occasions, I was given protection and fitted with a bulletproof vest. For example, at a "Cowboy/Logger Day Celebration" in Missoula, Montana, Representative Marlenee and I were both told that there was reason to be concerned for our safety. Authorities in Sweet Home, Oregon, fitted me with a bulletproof vest for my speech and my family was given protection on a tightly secured visit to the area.

Local authorities and the schools worked out a system to remove my children to a safe house when a threat was made.

Our home, located in a sparsely populated area twelve miles south of our small town, was given additional security by the local state patrolmen. We got a large dog. We put security systems in our home. We went for periods of time where our children were not allowed to answer the phone for fear of them getting a direct link to the lunacy.

The impact of these acts upon my family have been marked. When the threats started, my four children were aged three through twelve. We held numerous family meetings to determine whether or not we should continue our involvement in the debate over our future. We sought and got family and pediatric therapy to help deal with the stress. We relied heavily upon our minister. The decision of my family was always the same. Faced with shutting up, or speaking out and becoming a highly visible target, we chose to speak.

My family is not the only family in America who has felt this terror. There are many who elect to "shut up," and I will never judge or disagree with that decision. Yet there are some who have and continue to speak. Cathi Peterson, a skidder operator in the Sierra Nevada, has been a victim. Dean Bryant of Blue Ridge, Georgia, has had threats and equipment sabotage disrupt his family business of logging. Candy Boak of Willow Creek, California, has given up her pro-timber activities for fear of her life and that of her family. John Campbell, a timber industry executive from Scotia, California, has had his home firebombed.

Thankfully, the calls and threats have subsided over the years. I wish I could say the same about the feelings of terror in my family. I believe, I desperately want to believe, that the authorities are right and that the hate-mongers feel satisfied by making simple and idle threats. But, what if some self-anointed rambo of the eco-terror mindset acts upon a threat? And attacks more than just my logging equipment?

It is in this one small word - but - that the power of terrorism is real and palpable in my life. "But" and "what if" are horrifying thoughts to have when you are hundreds or thousands of miles away from home. As the father of four children, I will go to my grave wondering if I have made the right decisions. Should I have let the fanatics win and gone quietly about the business of letting them run roughshod over my civil liberties? That seems unthinkable. But I questioned the wisdom of that while, standing behind my six-year-old daughter, I wept quietly as I took the advice of the authorities and taught her and her siblings how to shoot.

*   *   *

Certainly not everyone who considers him or herself to be an environmentalist, or a participant in the environmental movement, is an eco-terrorist. Not everyone who disagrees with what the 'other side' is saying feels the need to 'shut them up.' Nor is everyone who participates in the environmental movement totally off their rocker. I, myself, profess to feel and have felt to be an environmentalist at heart! And over the years, I have met many sensible, good-hearted environmentalists.

Yet the environmental movement has most certainly changed from its early years of bipartisan support and well-intended legislation. So how did we get from there, to here? How did we get from a grassroots movement focused on awareness and education, to an ineffective mainstream movement feeding conflict and a radical group of outlying eco-terrorists who were emboldened and empowered to engage in violence and extremism of the worst kind?

In a nutshell, how did efforts towards the reasonable, in many cases, turn into efforts of insanity?

As alluded to earlier, the late 1960s and early to mid-1970s were powerful years in legislation. A few months prior to our first Earth Day, Congress passed the National Environmental Policy Act and gave citizens a voice in environmental decision-making. In the months following it, the Natural Resources Defense Council was established. Then President Nixon worked with Congress to create the Environmental Protection Agency (EPA). The National Oceanographic and Atmospheric Administration came into existence. A couple years later, the

Clean Water Act passed. The Marine Mammal Protection Act passed. DDT was banned in the United States. The Endangered Species Act was passed. President Nixon signed the Energy Supply and Environmental Coordination Act. The list goes on.

Republicans and Democrats worked together on legislation overseeing the environment. These were very productive years in terms of the growth and development of a movement. The Senate Environment and Public Works Committee, a bipartisan group, while frequently in disagreement with one another, did still get things done. Together they worked through some major accomplishments.

Yet cooperation diminished in the early 1980s. The loss of cross-party cooperation sparked an 'us versus them' mentality that led to a growth in extremes on both sides. And what started to emerge is what is now known, in some circles, as the, 'Big Green.' In other words, we saw the creation of what are now enormous, profit-driven non-governmental associations (NGOs) that live off of mainstream environmentalism and the donations they can compel or rustle up from their followers.

When President Reagan took office, he appointed James Watt, the leader of the Sagebrush Rebellion (a movement during the 1970s and 1980s that sought major changes to federal land control), as Secretary of the Interior. Watt took a strong pro-development stance and used his post to portray environmentalists as radicals outside the American mainstream. Yet his anti-environmentalist stance proved unpopular, as the American public still overwhelmingly supported environmental goals. As such, environmentalist organizations were able to play off of this frustration and sense of ostracism the American public felt at Watt's portrayal, and expanded their membership in response. Between 1980 and 1990, the Sierra Club's membership multiplied from 180,000 to 630,000, while the Wilderness Society's membership soared from 45,000 to 350,000. In 1983, Reagan was forced to replace Watt with a more moderate administrator, but by that time the damage had been done.

The 1980s also saw a splintering of the environmental movement itself. A number of radical environmentalist groups challenged the mainstream environmental organizations, claiming that they had become centralized bureaucracies 'out of touch' with the grassroots and were too willing to compromise the environmental agenda. One of the groups to make this challenge was Earth First!, which appeared on the national scene in 1981.

Earth First! was a big voice for eco-terror. The clenched, raised fist became their logo and their slogan of 'No Compromise in Defense Of Mother Earth' their rally cry. Earth First! employed a variety of radical tactics, including direct action, civil disobedience, guerilla theater and "ecotage," the sabotage of equipment used for clear cutting, road-building and dam construction. They had 'cells' of direct action activists located throughout the country with concentrations in the west. They put out a periodical called the *Earth First! Journal* that was published using presses at the University of Montana and they were very active on and off campuses. Dave Foremen was their titular leader and was a longtime friend of Edward Abbey who wrote the book on direct action against natural resource industries called <u>The Monkeywrench Gang</u>. Edward Abbey was revered by those who believed that compromise concerning environmental issues was leading to the death of our planet.

Dave Foreman followed Edward Abbey's book with a one-inch thick how-to on committing eco-terror, alluded to earlier, called <u>Eco-Defense: A Field Guide to Monkeywrenching</u>. The guide gives step-by-step instructions on how commit acts of terror. The book includes sections on toppling power lines, tipping over billboards, sabotaging airplanes so that they fall from the sky, blowing up heavy equipment used in building roads or in logging, pounding metal spikes into trees and much, much more. While the foreword states that it is 'for entertainment purposes only,' there have been thousands of eco-terrorists that have followed the book to the letter. In fact, there were yearly 'Rendezvous' held around the country where they provided field camp learning experiences to perfect the tactics explained in the book.

Foreman states that when there are folks in the hinterland committing these acts of terror, the more mainstream group requests such as removing roads, dams and discontinuing logging look reasonable in the overall scale of things. They proudly provide 'the radical edge' of the discussion so others can carve out a middle that is more in line with the far left. Further, Foreman states that by taking these actions they may be able to make it impossible for those who work in industry to get insurance covering their equipment or their jobs.

The *CBS* show "60 Minutes" became interested in eco-terror when the *Earth First! Journal* printed an article calling on people with terminal diseases (aids, cancer, etc) to not go out with a wimper, but a bang. They called upon the terminally ill to strap bombs on themselves and, as an exit from this earth, take with them a building, a dam or an industrial robotoid (human). They even had a list that they called the 'Eco-Fuckers Hit List' and gave names of those that they thought should be targeted for their crimes against mother earth.

Some eco-terrorists made international news. Ted Kaczyinski, the Unabomber, targeted as his third victim a friend of mine, Gil Murray of the California Forestry Association.[2] The intended target, Bill Dennison, had recently retired from his position with the association and had been replaced by Gil. Gil was a wonderful man, the father or two young boys, and was killed by a bomb he opened at his office in 1995. When the Unabomber was apprehended in 1996, the federal government began focusing on the reality of eco-terror cells acting in our nation and started arresting the perpetrators. Thankfully, shortly after the Unabomber was apprehended and the federal government started taking eco-terror seriously, the calls against me and my family largely stopped.

---

[2] Controversy remains over claims that Ted Kacynski targeted his victims off of an Earth First! hit list. While he has been linked to Earth First!, it is unclear whether or not his targets were a result of their materials and influence.

Chapter 10: Equal Access to 'Justice'

In the 1990s, Jasper Carlton notified the Kootenai National Forest about his desire to see all forest management halted. He had a vision for the future of the area. It was going to be an international park straddling the border between the United States and Canada. The park, which he dubbed, 'Columbia Mountains Peace Park,' would *not* include human management.

To achieve his vision, he said he was going to begin filing lawsuits representing species under the Endangered Species Act. The American taxpayers were going to pay for it, too. For years now, American taxpayers have been quietly providing millions of dollars of monetary support to groups perpetuating abuse of a well-intended statute, Equal Access to Justice (EAJ). EAJ was enacted in the late 1970s in an effort to level the legal playing field for the Vietnam Veterans who were trying to tackle the Veteran's Administration over sicknesses brought home by use of Agent Orange during the war. If an individual felt he or she was being or could be harmed by a federal action, the citizen was given the right to bring action against the federal government. The litigant could choose whichever federal court they liked (judge shop) and if the bench believed the litigant brought a reasonable question before the court, the judge could demand that the taxpayer pick up the tab for the litigant's court costs and attorney fees. The fees were either exacted from the agency being taken to task, or secured from an off-budget pot of money called the Judgment Fund.

This well-meaning law was amended during the Reagan administration to include non-governmental organizations (NGOs) representing individuals or groups who claim damage or potential damage from a federal action. Environmental attorneys nationwide saw the potential in questioning environmental actions proposed by land-managing federal agencies. The spotted owl lawsuits brought against federal land managers on the West Coast were just the beginning. Today, this act wreaks havoc on resource decision making whenever a federal nexus is involved.

Carlton's lawsuits were intended to halt all human management as well as yield a paycheck for his him and his group. The first lawsuit was going to be for protection of the grizzly bear. It was to be filed by the group he represented, the Fund for Animals. If that lawsuit did not work, he indicated he had a line-up of species: the bank hugging monkey flower, the Coeur D'Alene Salamander, the bastard flax, northern caribou and more. He was serious. And our society had given him a well-intended law, the Endangered Species Act, to misuse on his quest for his vision and another, Equal Access to Justice, to pay for his efforts.

I live in the Kootenai National Forest. That very first lawsuit raised question with me. If Jasper Carlton, from his home a thousand miles away in Boulder, Colorado, was really concerned about the grizzly bear, he would have favored forest management. Grizzly bears can run at 35 miles per hour, but only in short spurts. A fire in the northern Rockies can burn as fast as the wind blows for as long as it blows.

Unmanaged forests, as we will see later, create unhealthy forests ripe for disastrous, havoc-wreaking and ecosystem-damaging fires. Carlton had worked, earlier in his career, for the United States Forest Service (USFS) in north Idaho and the northwestern Montana area. Surely he knew that proper management enhanced, rather than hurt, the chances for these species? For millennium they relied on Native Americans' periodic management to maintain resilient, healthy forests.

Yet his goal was not to protect the twelve endangered species on his bucket list of lawsuits, but to stop logging and forest management and, I suspect, to support a funding stream through EAJ. His true sentiments became painfully clear a few years later.

During the hot, dry summer of 1994, an August lightning storm started 195 fires in a ring around Libby. From my window one evening, I saw a lightning strike start a fire above my best friend Ed's house. My heart skipped a beat. He was just across the highway, only about a half-mile away.

Knowing that you normally cannot see fires in the forest when it is on a hillside of close proximity behind your home, I jumped in my pickup and raced toward Ed's house. I never made it. I met him at the mailbox at the end of the driveway. He jumped out of his pickup and starting shouting and pointing at the hill behind MY house.

'Fire!' he yelled, and I turned to see the flames licking the sky on Paul Bunyan's Grave, the mountain behind my home.

We separated and tore back to our respective emergencies. My family spent a few frantic hours successfully stopping the fire from burning the mountain and our home. We were one of many, many families fighting fire that night.

The USFS called for help from all corners of the nation. Soon we had several thousand firefighters located in camps around town prepared to save the community and transport people from the fire area if needed. During this time, our local paper called Jasper Carlton in his Colorado home. They asked him for his opinion on the fire situation consuming the thoughts and prayers of the people of Libby. I will never forget his words.

"Fire," Carlton said to the reporter, "is a better manager than man. I would rather see it burn to the ground than have it logged."

To this day, I can't shake those words. And what's worse,

Jasper's goal soon yielded much of his desired result.

Forest management on the Kootenai National Forest began to be bogged down by litigation in the mid 1990s. Serial litigation groups from Montana and states far away have joined the gravy train of EAJ, while the American taxpayer and our forests pay a dear price.

The USFS admitted that much of the collapse of management planning was due to changing requirements concerning grizzly habitat, being driven both by litigation from NGOs and by consultation with the United States Fish and Wildlife Service (the very agency that assured the public management would not be impacted by simply having bears).

The consequences have been far-reaching and destructive; not just to the habitat, but to people.

*   *   *

Equal Access to Justice is just a small part of the funding stream necessary to keep initiatives, organizations and groups focused on conflict thriving. The majority of the capital needed to fund this industry is generated by focusing on or manifesting a fear-enabling crisis.

We assume that people facing problems wish to see those problems resolved. But is that indeed true for everyone? In many cases, which are outlined in various ways, through countless examples and with varying verbiage in texts, stories and everyday life, people often need conflict in order to continue to exist in the same manner in which they currently are. Who among us cannot think of at least one acquaintance who we might 'accuse' of perpetuating conflict in order to continue to talk about that same issue or to continue to be bothered by that same person?

All of us are likely guilty to some degree of perpetuating conflict, albeit small or minor conflicts, to enable our own existence as the more 'correct' individual. Rather than getting to the heart of the matter and resolving the conflict, in many cases, we allow and even feed conflicts such that they are perpetuated indefinitely. We come to say things like, "that person *always* insults me," and then, lo-and-behold, we feel validated when we do indeed feel insulted by that person.

Every fighter needs a cause. And, perhaps more than a cause, every fighter needs an opponent. One cannot simply solve the problem at hand and then continue on as they had before. The problem is gone! And if one's existence depends on problems then, once the problem at hand had been resolved, one would need to find a new cause or adversary in order to continue the fight. Even those fighting worthy battles for good causes (or at least causes generally regarded by large segments of the population as worthy or good) need to have an opponent or antagonist of some kind.

In other words, without a problem and without a villain, it is extremely hard to muster and motivate the troops. More to the point as it relates to natural resource industries in rural America, it is extremely hard to motivate others to support your cause with resources, especially cold hard cash, if there is not a worthy war that needs to be waged and fought. The direr the situation, the more punishing the outcome if one were to 'lose.' And the more infuriating the opponent, the easier it seems to motivate financial support from do-gooders and members of the well-intentioned public.

The inability to continue on, as normal, once a challenge has been conquered is never so true as for those employed in the industry of conflict itself. Conflicts have long given support for entire industries, with legal and regulatory professionals (lawyers come to mind) taking the brunt of the jokes to this end.

However, lawyers are generally expected to be conducting themselves in the confines of the law or judiciary system. In brutal terms, one would consider lawyers to be fighting their opponents with some sort of oversight by referees (if not people, then the system itself).

Far more concerning than legal battles fought in the court of law or within the government or legal system are battles being waged in the "courts of popular opinion," through media, in public settings or in the social realm. Battles being waged between warring parties, sparring for the win in terms of popular opinion, are worrisome because they are battles fought without the confines or boundaries of the judiciary or legal systems. One can wage war and argue their points without any mind to actual facts; indeed, the proliferation of fake news even with respect to issues as important as the United States' national elections has been a major concern in recent times. Taking to Facebook and Twitter to garner support, including financial, for one's cause allows a group to present themselves in whatever light they prefer, unfettered by inconvenient facts.

Perhaps those groups or individuals thriving on conflicts in the world, masquerading as do-gooders, exist on both sides. In many cases, it is hypothesized that the do-gooders themselves are blind to their need for conflict. However, for a group that is funded to take on a cause, it goes without saying that the funding stream would dry up if it were announced that the cause was no longer worthy (perhaps because the problem had been solved, thus resolving the conflict surrounding said issue).

Yet an activist organization seeking to save something, say the waters or some species of wildlife, exists so long as the waters or wildlife need saving. So what begins as a positive endeavor with likely well-intentioned leadership and well-intentioned supporters (and funders) evolves, quite naturally, into an organization that *requires* conflict for its survival.

In order to remain in operation, conflict must exist because the group itself needs a reason to exist. In order to thrive, grow and prosper, in all likelihood the group needs increasingly dire causes against which to battle. What begins as a well-meaning and positive endeavor can evolve into a perverse situation where groups exist because of, and profit off of, conflict.

Chapter 11: Bears & the Consumer Paradox

The name, doing nothing but rolling off the tongue, sounds ominous. The facts and folklore of the animal seem to lend credence to the fear, causing goose pimples to run up your arm if you are in the forests of northwest Montana and hear a noise that could be a snowshoe rabbit or...THE bear. The GRIZZLY bear. Ursus Arctos Horibilis.

Growing up in those forests, I was long aware that we shared our patch of earth with this noble creature. I was aware that care needed to be taken when entering those areas where the bear was king. In fact, coexistence with 'the bear' is part of the romance of living in Montana.

Yet this romantic notion has not always been commonplace. The grizzly bear was treated as a threat to human habitation for over a century as man carved out homes in the prairie and forest landscapes and infringed on the bear's territory. Many were killed by the pioneers in an effort to protect lives and property. Such an act was not illegal and was accepted by society as a necessary step in subduing the wilderness and making the land hospitable for people.

For thousands of years, the Native Americans revered the animal for its prowess and majesty. But they, too, had a long history of killing it when deemed necessary. During these early days, however, the bear did not live primarily in forested regions. Rather, the bear's prime habitat included those areas where food was plentiful. Unlike their coastal cousins who rely upon fish to build their fat inventory, the inland populations of the Rocky Mountains subsist mainly upon berries, bugs, roots of certain plants and carrion. Prime areas for grizzly bears were in central Montana where the Great Plains meet the mountains.

In the early 1900s, the state of Montana decided the grizzly bear was a game animal and management of the species included harvesting of a limited number through the sale of hunting licenses. Having a grizzly bear as part of your hunting repertoire was considered to be quite an honor. The loss of habitat on the plains, coupled with extermination efforts and hunting pressures, caused a decrease in the number of bears that coincided with President Nixon signing the Endangered Species Act into law on December 28, 1973. As such, by the time I moved back to Montana from college in 1984, the grizzly bear had been listed as a threatened species under this act (1975). Hunting seasons had been halted. Planning was underway to set up habitat and species management regimes to stop the decline of the bear's population throughout its historic range in Montana.

Libby is surrounded by nearly 2.5 million acres of United States Forest Service (USFS) lands. Management of those lands is required to take into consideration the recovery needs of threatened and endangered animals. The grizzly bear's specific needs were folded into the 1985 Forest Plan that was completed for the Kootenai National Forest.

Some recovery efforts had already been undertaken before the forest planning process began, but these efforts had been haphazard. They included the transfer of 'problem' bears from the Glacier Park area to our more remote and less populated landscape. They were caught and transported to the forests of northwest Montana and unceremoniously dumped into the brush or, in other words, my home.

Problem bears were those who had become habituated to human things like garbage. Back then, in a misguided effort to give tourists a close-up and personal look at the grizzly, some national park folks had been encouraging bears to come close to their visitors by dumping garbage near their chalets. Though the park had a rule against this baiting, the rule was seldom enforced and baiting worked quite well in attracting bears. It also facilitated situations that spawned the first of many fatal encounters with the bear in or near our parks, including the killing of two girls in separate places by separate bears, which spawned the non-fiction bestseller *The Night Of The Grizzly* by Jack Olsen.

In the spring of 1988, the United States Fish and Wildlife Service announced the conclusion of a planning process that would ultimately yield a recovered population of grizzly bears in the Cabinet/Yaak ecosystem (my home area). The Fish and Wildlife Service and USFS assured the public that the recovery process would have no impact on them and their interaction with the national forest. The 1985 Forest Plan included multiple-use management guidelines and had all the provisions needed to manage necessary habitat for a recovered population of bears. The only thing missing from the plan, they assured us, were the bears themselves.

In late winter of 1988, a headline in our local press caught my attention: 'Grizzly Bears to be Augmented in the Cabinet/Yaak Ecosystem.' This announcement raised some questions amongst myself and other members of our community. What, for instance, is the Cabinet/Yaak Ecosystem? What is augmentation, exactly? What does this mean for those of us who live here?

A public meeting was arranged in the local high school gymnasium to help the public understand what the Fish and Wildlife Service was proposing. My wife PJ and I attended that meeting, and boy did that meeting change our lives. We were informed that augmentation was the artificial reintroduction of bears into our ecosystem and it was to continue until the grizzly bear population was recovered.

Augmentation efforts included some interesting methods, including simple transfers of bears from other ecosystems. The bears to whom we were going to provide a home were largely coming from just north of us in British Columbia, Canada. They have a large grizzly population in Canada. They were still hunting the bear, and removal of a few of their bears wouldn't impact the bear's population dynamics. So we were told.

Understandably, we had questions about the quantity of bears proposed to be placed in our area. Dr. Chris Servheen, who we learned was the grizzly recovery coordinator for Planet Earth, informed us that since we had a historic population of grizzly bears the agency was required by law to recover the species back to its historic levels. We inquired with Dr. Servheen as to the historical population. He gave us what was to become a fairly common answer, "We have no idea."

What were they going to do if they had no concept of historic parameters? "We must have a viable genetic pool of bears that can thrive without human interaction." What was a genetically viable population level? "We have no idea." However, Dr. Servheen said that the goal was to have 90 to 120 bears in the area to begin delisting it as no longer threatened.

This number of 90 to 120 bears meant little to us. Is that a lot? A little? Answers to these questions, and the relative concern that the answers would bring, depended upon the current population of grizzly bears in our area. We were obviously already living with the bear and having little problem but we knew nothing about our current population level. We asked Dr. Servheen, "How many currently live here?" We got, of course, the now familiar answer of, "We have no idea," followed with, "We think that there are 4 of them."

PJ, being raised in California and not Montana, had concerns that extended beyond those of us Montana-raised folks. If we have four grizzlies in our backyard, she summarized, and you are going to dump 116 more of them into that same yard, is that going to be a problem? Posted in the gym was a map of the Kootenai National Forest with the areas considered grizzly habitat denoted in a variety of colors in order of importance and priority. It looked like someone had thrown an octopus at the map with habitat arms running around the forest. Those arms were, in places, less than two miles wide. Grizzly bears can have a 50-mile eating radius. In between some of these arms of habitat were the places many people live, including us.

PJ stood in front of the map and found our home and our property. We live 12 miles south of Libby at the junction where Libby Creek leaves the rugged mountains and enters the valley floor. She found that the grizzly habitat immediately surrounding the Cabinet Mountains and butting up to our home's area was hatch-marked on the map. When she asked what the hatched area meant she was startled to learn that it marked 'the human grizzly conflict zone.' That sounded bad. If not bad, it definitely didn't sound good. With growing trepidation, she then inquired if we could still live there. Certainly, she was told. Could we continue to send our children into the yard or out back to fish in the creek without worrying about them getting consumed? Certainly, she was told.

Well, certainly, but we may want to consider modifying our behaviors a bit. Those modifications, learned through years of grizzly co-habitation in the national parks, include such things as going in groups into forested areas and making noise to alert and scare off the bears. She was told that we may want to consider doing what park tourists do, and tie little bells onto our children's shoes and walking sticks before sending them out and about. That way, the bears would hear the bells and run away. They assured her that if there was ever a bad bear, a 'problem' bear, that the agency would deal with the issue and remove it from our area. It was clear to us that the difference between a 'good' bear and a 'bad' bear was easy to discern. 'Bad' bears have bells in their poop.

As we asked our tough questions, the agency personnel became more and more agitated by our seeming lack of understanding for their cause. We were finally informed again that the Endangered Species Act required that places with a historic population of bears must, and would be, part of the statute required recovery process. The agency was there to tell us how that was going to be accomplished. They were not there, we were informed, to take a public opinion poll.

We objected. Vigorously. While we were forming our Citizen Group, the Fish and Wildlife Service sent the Assistant Director to Libby to see what the commotion was about. He and I were having coffee at Henry's Café (if you come to Libby, you have coffee at Henry's Café...) and discussing the community's concerns. I reiterated to him the questions on the minds of those who live here. Primarily, I asked why the agency decided that a top-down, command-and-control effort designed from afar was being pursued rather than sitting and working with us. He repeated the mantra that we had heard from Dr. Servheen when he said, 'you have a historic population of grizzly bears here and under the endangered species act we are required to recover that population back to its historic levels.'

Walking down the logical trail of 'you have a historic population therefore we must restore,' I asked him if he had ever seen the California state flag. He had. I asked him what was smack in the middle of that flag, and he responded 'the golden bear.' It certainly is in the middle of that state's flag and is, in fact, the California state animal. The Golden Bear is a silver tipped grizzly. That state has a history of grizzly bears. I then asked the next logical question: 'When you are done in Libby, are you going to do Sacramento next?'

At first he looked shocked, then laughed, and leaned forward in his chair and whispered, 'can you imagine the public outcry?'

I could.

*   *   *

Recovering the grizzly bear, in quite specific locales, underscores a constant paradox concerning the environment and our need to consume in order to survive. People want bears to have homes. They want endangered animals to thrive and their populations to grow. And just like people want animals to be saved, they also want things. They even want the economic benefits of producing those things.

Take, for instance, the current focus on reviving manufacturing sectors in the United States and production "at home." We like the jobs that are created from production. And we like to claim the benefits those workers have on the local economy as they secure housing, pay taxes to support local infrastructure and schools and buy goods from retailers. Beyond the physical goods these new workers consume, and the physical structures they support (playgrounds and parks being a favorite), they also use services. These workers support their households with plumbers, electricians, construction firms and even home decorators. The workers themselves go to doctors, dentists and use various other self-maintenance industries. Fees are paid to real estate agents. The list goes on. When a worker relocates into your town to take a newly created job, we are excited about that job. We are more than happy to have the positive impacts of production in our locale.

Sometimes people are even willing to redefine their locale to claim production activities. Chatter that starts with "produced in the USA" migrates to "produced in North America." Because aside from the obvious benefits of production, there is a sense of pride. There is the pride in production and having created. This also drives human beings to wish to be a part of the creation of goods (and services, although services are more mobile in today's economy).

What people also and most certainly do want, as mentioned, are the actual things that production gives us. Things are great. Presents of clothes and shoes are lovely. New cars have that special and coveted new car smell. And what child is not surrounded by heaps of brightly colored plastic? Babies, in fact, often come accompanied with tons of plastic goods. And, oh, the electronics. There is always the newer edition of your laptop, desktop, tablet or phone that is released seemingly immediately after you obtained your last device. You are practically being begged to upgrade said devices every time you turn around. New devices mean more production of electronics parts, touch screens and plastic casings.

Yet despite all these things we want, such as the goods and the certain positive benefits of production, we don't want any of the negative aspects associated with the production of our many products. Nobody likes the negative impacts of production in their neighborhood. Ask any resident how they enjoy haze and smog, traffic backed up for miles and miles in gridlocked congestion and waterways that are unusable for recreational purposes (let alone for consumption without substantial treatment, which in turn requires those tax dollars to be contributed towards infrastructure and maintenance). Production of our much-coveted "computer guts," for instance, comes with negative impacts on someone, somewhere. And therein lies our paradoxical relationship with the systems surrounding production and consumption.

A paradox is, per dictionary.com, "a statement or proposition that seems self-contradictory or absurd but in reality expresses a possible truth." Or, "any person, thing, or situation exhibiting an apparently contradictory nature." So, hmmm … I want goods, but I don't want what comes along with all this business of production. I want electricity at the switch, immediate and cheap… I just don't want a coal-fired plant, a nuclear plant, a solar farm, a dam or a windmill anywhere near me. Oh, and I don't want to look at a power line either. I want my food to be abundant, safe, pretty and… cheap. I just don't like the processes of soil management, pesticide management, nutrient management or biotechnology. I like my diamond ring, it is just mining I hate. I love wooden furniture, it is just stumps that suck. So how, exactly, do you suppose the goods we so crave come into existence?

Not in my backyard, or aptly called NIMBY, is a commonly used term to express opposition to any undesired elements sitting near one's residence or new civic projects. For instance, individuals desire community services and amenities, such as garbage and recycling facilities. But NIMBY is a near universal desire to have that necessary amenity located away from your own residence. Although, of course, it should still be within a reasonable distance so it can provide your service in a convenient fashion.

In other words, I want my garbage to be picked up and disposed of in an orderly and timely fashion, but I don't want to smell or see the garbage dump. And actually, while I'm at it, I prefer not to see too much truck traffic, especially not garbage trucks (which begs the question of how trash should be transported to the far away dump). Beyond the obvious need for some tradeoff in garbage dump location between close and far away, the more fatal flaw exists in the fact that the garbage dump (or jail or other less desirable item) needs to be located somewhere. And this means that it will be located near some*one*.

Everyone can agree that a garbage dump is necessary and thus needs a location. In other cases, we can also all agree that a certain project is necessary and consequently needs to be located somewhere. We all remain fine with these universally accepted truths, so long as the location chosen is not in my backyard!

Our urge to locate unpleasant facilities or those with negative impacts, such as odors, environmental challenges or unpleasing aesthetics, far away extends well beyond just civic projects. Think about any type of desired or necessary production. Then think about the location of that production. Or what about the land set aside from production, lands that are specifically protected? Perhaps these lands are protected from logging, hunting or are protected to preserve a habitat for animals which we, as a society, would like to see preserved or saved – but our individual support for this protection evaporates if the land in question is used by us for a purpose disallowed by the proposed protection.

Saving bears sounds great. Enabling bears' reproduction so there is a larger population also sounds great, particularly if you feel an affinity towards wildlife and wish to see wildlife populations preserved. But where should those bears live? Do you want them to live in your backyard? Well, perhaps you would like to see them saved somewhere in North America, which seems close enough to be meaningful (in the spirit of claiming production close to home), but far enough away that they pose no danger to my dog in the backyard (or child for that matter).

So we desire goods, including the piles of plastics and consumer electronics. These goods are produced somewhere, and somewhere nearby that somewhere, there are residents facing the negative consequences of such production. Yet as the consumer of goods, how many of those negative consequences do you actually see? The answer depends on where you live. But given the vast diversity of products that most of us in society consume regularly, the response is likely 'not many.'

Therein lies the paradox of production. We want the goods, but we don't want them to be produced. More specifically, we don't want to incur the costs, largely nonmonetary, of their production. People in both urban and rural settings share similar reactions. It's just the same with our civic projects. We want them close enough to service our needs or desires but let's keep them far enough away so I don't suffer negative consequences of the byproducts of production, such as noise or stink, for example.

Factories can create smog, water pollution and traffic. Livestock operations can create water pollution or even truck traffic, not to mention the foul odors. By biological process, chickens, pigs, sheep, goats and cattle produce manure and excrement. But most of us like to eat our meat, thus necessitating livestock production and the existence of farms housing livestock animals. The existence, you say, is not the problem (for the majority of people), but it's the site selected. Simply allow the placement of such, potentially offensive, facilities away from me. Well, the problem is that 'away from you' generally means nearer to someone else.

Local siting decisions are rather simple to imagine. Does the new livestock facility locate on this side of the mile section of ground or on the opposite side? Does the new plant locate north or south of the highway? Does a manufacturing plant locate within 1 mile or 10 miles of the new housing development? The conversation becomes more difficult when considering the global exchange of goods and global trade partners. If you want random plastic household goods, for argument's sake, but don't want the environmental impacts associated with production near your home, then the production facility may be forced to locate further away. What does further away mean in this case? Across state lines? In another country? The relocation of production does not eliminate the negative aspects of production. It just relocates them.

To borrow from common political arguments surrounding manufacturing, manufacturers will relocate to where there are more favorable conditions, which generally means less stringent regulations. Consider, for a moment, whether the geographical relocation of the plant is the only thing likely to take place. Said plant is unlikely to relocate and conform to standards that are stricter than necessary. This costs money. Basically, you're not going to get the exact same plant in Locale B as it originally was in Locale A.

Imagine a plant is relocating somewhere with less environmental regulations. We can expect that the plant will be rebuilt to these lower standards. They'll match the requirements of the locale. So speaking purely with regard to the total environmental impact of that single plant, the relocation did not simply *move* the environmental impact, but it actually (potentially) *increased* the impact.

This isn't always the case. However, if it is generally preferred that production will take place *not in my backyard*, then it will have to take place nearer to someone else. Will that movement actually lessen or increase the total negative impact of production? Given economic forces at work, production won't likely happen in places where regulations are more stringent since the cost of compliance will generally increase as strictness of compliance increases. Production will chase the path of least resistance (at least in this wildly oversimplified example).

Simply speaking, if you do not want the trees in your country cut down or logged, but you desire wood furniture, the world market will bring you wood furniture from sources outside your country. Will that wood be harvested more or less sustainably than if it was harvested in your home country? Probably less, but the more accurate response is "it depends" in most cases. Not all firms produce using equivalent processes, regardless of physical location.

Yet what remains steadfast is the need to appreciate the consumer paradox... if you want goods (and services), it seems that there will need to be production of those goods. You want goods, thus you need production, thus you have a problem.

Just so, if you want grizzly bear populations to rise, someone's got to pay the price for it. And have you thought through who it's going to impact and how they might feel about it? There are people who are going to have to tie bells around their kids' shoelaces because 116 bears are being relocated to their backyard. Would you be willing to do so without having been given a voice at the table and due consideration? The 116 bears, recall, are joining the 4 already living there. Of course, also recall, 'bad' bears, identified by bell-poop, will be dealt with (whatever that means).

This paradox is particularly troubling for Americans as members of the most consumptive society on earth. Is our legacy going to be one in which we love to consume, but do not want to produce, and therefore relegate production to developing countries that have abundant resources, burgeoning populations, a heavy need for cash and the economic inability to be environmentally sensitive? Will we settle on importing raw products from countries using methods we quit using thirty years ago, just so we do not have to pay the price of production on a local level?

Production and conservation are complex. For each desire we have, for goods or for preservation, there will be some trade-off. And these tradeoffs can become problems, problems which will require cooperation and communication to tackle, as the answer will require compromise and a give-and-take – regardless of where you happen to lay your head.

Chapter 12: Smokey Bear

Flames pierced the sky. Red and orange lapping tongues of fire ate up the land. Clouds of scorching ash swept through towns and villages. A trail of blackened, flattened forests trailed in its wake. The raging wildfire voraciously ripped a path of destruction across the land, a brutal reminder of the raw power of nature.

It was 1910. A severe drought had set the Western states of Idaho, Montana and Washington on a knife's edge that summer. The customary heavy rains of the region failed to arrive that spring. And from April all the way through May, June, July and most of August, increasingly nervous residents watched as barely a drop struck the progressively dry and barren earth.

Then on July 23rd, dark clouds gathered on the horizon. Rangers, miners and families watched nervously. The air tingled with charged air as the storm wind rushed past their houses and front stoops. Cracks of thunder shook the earth and flashes of brilliant lightening lit the sky. Yet the anticipated rain did not fall. The terrible occurrence had come to pass; a dry electrical storm. Lightning strikes, but not a drop of moisture.

Hundreds of lightning bolts shot down on the dried out timberlands again and again over the coming weeks. Thousands of fires ignited across the states. Men, mostly immigrants, were recruited as firefighters and troops deployed. By August 19th, these groups had extinguished three thousand fires and controlled the ninety largest. Working conditions were brutal. With no electricity or machinery, everything had to be done by hand. Exhausted, they could only hope desperately that the end was nigh.

Then the worst possible weather phenomenon struck. A fierce wind, hot, dry and near hurricane-force, blew in from the Southwest. With raging force, it shrieked across the states. Like warm breath blown across tinder to start a campfire, nature did the same on a magnified scale and within hours the land was ablaze.

In less than two days, three million acres of land were destroyed. Scores of people were dead by fire, smoke and falling trees. Clouds of ash and smoke blackened the sky across the northern United States and southern Canada. In Cheyenne temperatures dropped to 38 degrees, in Denver they plummeted 19 degrees in ten minutes.

*   *   *

Trees are really just tubes of carbon. The carbon is sequestered in the tree body during the photosynthesis process. The tree takes in carbon dioxide, holds the carbon and releases oxygen. One can enter a forest with logging equipment, remove some of these tubes of carbon and ship them to a processing plant. There they can be turned into consumable products for our consuming society; boards, plywood, paper, furniture and sawdust pellets for heating our homes, schools and businesses.

In many areas, forests today have now become so thick that the tree tops touch in what is called a 'forest canopy.' As the canopy closes, the sunlight that has heretofore been able to reach the forest floor and invigorate an abundance of life forms is cut off. The grasses and berries that could, and should, have grown in the forested areas are far less abundant than before the canopy closure. As a result, creatures such as the grizzly bear, who rely upon the forest floor for sustenance, are slowly being choked out of their homes.

Worse yet, however, is the fact that trees are water pumps. A full-sized pine tree can suck two or three hundred gallons of water per day out of the aquifer and transpire it into the air. This transpiration is what gives forest areas the feeling of being 'cool.' Yet when there are too many trees fighting for a finite quantity of water, the trees become weak. The stressed trees emit a pheromone that is a sure signal to naturally-occurring bugs like the northern pine beetle that the tree is prime for attack. A healthy tree will be able to fight off a bug attack by exuding copious amounts of sap into the holes drilled into the bark by the bug intruder (this is where the term 'pitch' comes from since healthy trees literally 'pitch' the bugs out). A weakened tree cannot win the battle with the bug and is killed. When entire forests are overstocked with too many 'water pumps,' they are prime targets for massive insect infestations. Such an infestation has been decimating the forests of the Rocky Mountains for several decades.

As alluded to earlier, Native American populations managed the forests with controlled, periodic burns for millennia. Now, with the removal of Native American management, trees that had for eons been killed when they were two feet tall in intermittent fires are now free to grow. And grow they have.

The organic materials that now lay in wait for removal by fire is called the 'fuel load' by fire specialists. When the 'fuel loading' is light, fires do good things like invigorate topsoil with the infusion of minerals, promote the growth of things like huckleberry bushes, kill little trees that will compete for sustenance if allowed to grow and pop open the heat sensitive cones of the lodgepole pine trees to provide seeds for nature's next generation of forest. When 'fuel loading' is too heavy, however, the fires do bad things like climb up and into the canopy cover and burn entire trees rather than staying near the ground and scorching the trees bark, sterilize the topsoil down to bedrock, kill the living soil so that berries cannot or do not come back and incinerate the pine cones and their forest-regenerating seeds.

In 1889, the first modern-era 'fire season' of the post-Native American landscape took advantage of decades of fuel loading. It burned in giant swaths of stand-destroying blazes. Fires swept through and burned to the ground small towns like the ferry landing at Leonia in Montana along with bigger cities like Spokane, Washington.

Many thought that the fires of 1889 were nothing but a naturally occurring event that occasionally struck the forests of the area. This was partially true. Natural fire was and is a part of the northern Rocky Mountain ecosystem and has, in fact, defined much of the forest landscape's flora, fauna and wildlife. For instance, fire dependent and fire resistant trees of the area include the lodge pole pine. This fire dependent specie's heat-sensitive cones release seeds when they are heated and have long provided a rapid response post-fire cover crop.

What is not known, however, is what forests would look like without the influence of humans during the ten to fifteen thousand years between the end of the last mini-ice-ages and the arrival of western Europeans colonizers. What would a natural forest look like without the heavy hand of utilitarian management by fire employed by the Native Americans? Certainly there would still have been natural fires introduced each year through lightning ignitions. But the question of what 'natural' fire regimes would look like, without any human influence, is simply not known. Nor do we know exactly what the forest would look like today if European settlers had never set foot in the landscape.

We do know that the fires of 1889 were large and burned a great deal of the landscape in one particularly rough season. We also know that the snags left behind during those fires suffered root loss, fell to the forest floor and provided the setting for the conflagration of 1910. The fire of 1910 occurred some 80 years after the removal of Native American management and was a result of some 80 years of 'fuel' accumulation in the Inland Northwest. It was, as we saw, a summer noted for its heat and a lack of rain that culminated in a fire-storm of epic proportions. The fires were so large that the people of Montreal Canada called 1910 the 'Summer Without A Sun' because our orb of life turned dark orange from the plumes of smoke circling the globe and stayed orange until the snows of winter cleared the air. Nature was cleaning up a mess in the forest.

The fires of 1910 happened just four short years after the federal government, under President Teddy Roosevelt, had formed the United States Forest Service (USFS), the Bureau of Land Management and set aside undeveloped lands to be managed for the public's interest within the federal forest reserve. The move was made in an effort to protect the forests from overharvesting and to assure that they would be around for all future generations of Americans. When the public realized the extent of the damage caused by the largest fire in recorded history, they were incensed. The pressure was on to 'save the forests' from fires. Smokey the Bear became a mainstay that symbolized the public's desire to keep the forests from burning to the ground. The forest managing agencies became extremely efficient in putting fires out.

Forest scientists have long told us, however, that there is a downside to this efficient removal of fire from the forest ecosystems. The forest surrounding Libby and hundreds of communities in the west no longer have a 'good' fuel load. Around Libby, forests no longer have 50 or 60 trees to the acre. Across tens of thousands of acres, the average can be as many as 500 trees, and the trees are stressed. Many have been attacked and killed by beetles and other diseases. For the first time since forest inventories have been studied, the mortality in our national forests of the northern Rockies is outstripping the growth of the forest.

It is the hope of those in our area that corrective forest restoration can happen before the three-million-acre 1910 fire is recreated. We know that time is not on our side concerning this eventuality, as the forest that grew out of those two days of hell are largely nature's cover crop of lodge pole pine and 'old' for this species is around 100 years. This time the coming fires could be even worse, though, since we have another century of unimpeded forest growth stacked in the forest. The fuel loads are tremendous.

We have the potential for a 'Katrina of the Forest' event in the inland northwest. Much like how the experts in New Orleans knew the dikes would fail with a storm like Katrina, forest experts know that the forest could have a single event loss much like the 'Big Blow Out' of 1910. Yet when the fires burned in 1910, it is estimated that there was around 15,000 people living in the fire area. Highways and road systems were almost non-existent, but many people were able to escape the fires on the newly built logging-rail systems that traversed the area to aid in timber harvest.

Today, not only is our population much greater, but we have very, very few rail systems in place and though we have highways that serve the area, our roads zig-zag through heavily timbered areas and are not where you want to be during a fire-storm.

*   *   *

There are a few ways that forest density (fuel loading) can be reversed. We can, and sometimes are, purposely lighting fires to remove fuel. These 'controlled burns' can be coupled with mechanical removal of fuels (logging) to assure that the controlled fires are beneficial to the forest. We can and should be planning to maintain a safe, robust, resilient forest. Yet the exact opposite has happened. What gives?

On the Kootenai Forest, local stakeholders (many of whom were at war with each other twenty years ago) have worked to embrace forest restoration efforts. The challenge for the land manager is passing planning through the appeals and litigation process. The USFS spends an enormous amount of time and money trying to make their planning bulletproof for the ensuing court battles. Happily, the local agency personnel are good at their jobs and win most of their cases in court – but the time and resources sucked up in the process can mean that the wins in court are too little, too late for our overstocked forest. It isn't just the inland northwest at risk. In 2012, *NPR* ran a special series called 'Megafires: the new normal of the southwest." One of these episodes was called, "How The Smokey Bear Effect Led to Raging Wildfires." In it, journalist Christopher Joyce succinctly captures a piece of the story. After the 1910 fire, the forces at play called for an all-out ban on fires in the Southwest (as in other places in the United States), and thus evolved Smokey Bear, cautioning children and campers for decades to 'not start a fire!'

Yet Smokey wasn't getting it all right, as the Forest Service now admits. In their very own teaching guide for fourth graders, entitled, "What Smokey Bear Never Told You," they write, " We thought we were doing the right thing, keeping our forests nice and green. But, then scientists learned that fire actually plays an important role in the forest."

As fire expert Craig Allen, ecologist with the United States Geological Survey in New Mexico, is quoted as saying, we are now discovering that fire is increasingly out of our control. "Basically, the mountains in the Southwest — you can almost think of them as caskets of fuel," Allen says. "Gunpowder has been building up in these things for a century, and now it's dangerous to try to defuse."[3]

As this story highlights, managing our natural resources is complex. There is rarely, if ever, an easy 'soundbite' solution. Getting to the bottom of our natural resources 'truths' can be a long, winding path. And it is not one that lends itself well to today's information environment. With flashy headlines, quick soundbites and inflammatory messages capturing our attention for just a span of seconds, accessing a space of true learning is being challenged by the day.

Yet even prior to today's fast and quick information

[3] Joyce, C. (2012, August 23). How The Smokey Bear Effect Led To Raging Wildfires. Retrieved December 12, 2016, from
http://www.npr.org/2012/08/23/159373691/how-the-smokey-bear-effect-led-to-raging-wildfires

environment, pride, folly and political forces can and did lead to silly, damaging or downright wrong approaches towards our natural resources. There were people and experts back in 1910 and onward who called for periodic burns and who knew that this was the right course of action. Yet, for whatever mixture of wanting to do things 'differently' and desiring an easy message, the wrong course of action was rallied.

This will continue to be an element that must be considered at all times. Most groups, be they government, non-governmental association or corporation, don't tend to gravitate towards nuanced and complex explanations. The simpler and clearer, the better. Yet our natural resources and the environment are not simple. That the answers fall somewhere in a gradient of gray is almost assured. However, our messages still continue to pound home some version of black or white.

Getting the 'whole' story can be critical to deriving a reasonable stance or ensuring that a person is rallying behind the right cause. Yet the whole story is very rarely presented. It's much easier to say, 'no fires! Do your part!' than it is to say, "periodic and controlled burns or thinning is the best method for maintaining our healthy forests."

This desire for soundbite ready answers has been a serious enemy towards progress, not just one to which everyone else succumbs, but to which we ourselves often fall victim.

*   *   *

To see progress, it is important that we be critical towards all the information that is fed to us. Like journalists, we must become accustomed to checking our sources and making sure we're seeing all the sides. We can sit and engage in constructive, good-faith dialogues with those that have different opinions than ourselves. And then, only then, draw our own, reasoned conclusion while remaining open-minded to any new pieces of information we may garner along the way. This is incredibly challenging when Facebook and Twitter are the echo chambers for thoughts and opinions, and when we don't properly vet our news sources and trust blindly any old headline or talk show host proclaiming their 'opinion' as fact.

Information access will control the outcome, and while we must be dedicated, hardworking and patient in how we communicate with others, so must we be equally vigilant of the very information we, ourselves, consume. We can't afford any more Smokey Bear debacles to endanger our natural resources, our livelihoods and our homes.

Chapter 13: Loved, & Saved, to Death

Since the 1950s, Americans began to enjoy the fruits of an industrialized, capitalist economic boom. The vast majority of people were no longer just struggling to make ends meet, keep a roof over their families' heads and food on the table. The economic boom of the 1950s and 60s gave most middle class Americans an abundance of two things that were not common in the eons of human history that preceded them – time and money.

Previously, it was mainly the wealthy who had the time and financial ability to do things like travel and take vacations longer than a weekend. Leisure time was not common in agrarian-based cultures. And, the early history of industrialization certainly did not include two weeks of vacation time for workers in the factories and sweatshops.

But by the late 1950s, nearly everyone had found a little time to go exploring away from home. They had a little money to fund those travels, a car that could be relied upon to make it to and from a distant destination and an expanding interstate highway system that enhanced the travel experience. Hotels and motels started to pop up along the roadways that led out of the city and into the hinterland. Gas was cheap. Food was plentiful, and available anywhere they went.

In addition to this, the majority of society was, for the first time in history, living in urban and suburban areas rather than in rural areas. In fact, most people who were living in or near the cities were already a generation or two removed from the farming culture their parents or grandparents had left in order to seek a 'better life.' With the inclusion of television sets in nearly every living room, the increasingly urbanized society's connection to rural areas was no longer outside their living room door, but rather inside that square box with an antenna attached.

Our urban peers were staring at visions of environmental degradation being beamed across the land onto their television sets just as we in rural America were. With this new technology, they could see firsthand the environmental consequences of unregulated industry on their waterways and air. They joined in with the rest of us in our growing concern for the environment. And they rightfully cheered when we began to enact policies that would protect the environment.

As the urban population now represents over 80 percent of our society, and metropolitan districts have grown larger and larger and larger, for several decades now many have used their two weeks of summer vacation to escape what they themselves call their 'urban jungle.' There is a hunger to revisit the places their ancestors abandoned. There is a hunger to reconnect with the 'real' world of nature. Each year there are tens of millions who leave cities like Seattle to visit the Cascades or the rolling hills of the Palouse. They race out of Chicago to visit the Wisconsin Dells or the upper peninsula of Michigan. They drive or fly out of Los Angeles to walk among the glaciers of Glacier Park or the fountains of Yellowstone Park.

Not surprisingly, they fall in love with the places they are visiting. They love the clean air, clean water and abundant wildlife. For many it comes as a shock that these things still exist because, after all, they have been watching the supposed destruction of nature on the news and in movies since they were old enough to form a memory. Many truly believed that they were just gone, or ruined. And yet, they discover, here these things are right outside of their rental car window. AWESOME! The natural settings they drive or hike through look nothing like the areas from which they came. Lincoln County, Montana, looks not a bit at all like Chicago, or Seattle or Los Angeles. It is different, raw and seemingly wild.

We cannot blame people for their love of the places that we, rural Americans, get to call home. On the contrary, it is a love that we share and we should celebrate that. I know my sense of place runs deep in my blood. I love the Kootenai Valley and the Kootenai Forest. I love the snowcapped mountains, the crystal clear streams and lakes, the wildlife just outside my door. I love the sights, the sounds and the smells of the place I have called home. I have often reflected that it is a human thing, a part of our nature, to associate a bit of who we are with the place we are from.

Maybe if I were raised in the city, I would have the same molecular tug at the sights, sounds and smells of the urban landscape. But I was raised in the forest-blanketed mountains of the inland west. And it is this natural environment that is embedded in my DNA. So deeply is it embedded, in fact, that little things like the smell of the evergreens of home can make me weak-kneed if I have been away for too long. Just as a farmer can tell the difference between his soil and soil from other areas, I can tell the difference between the smell of my forest and others I visit. During my years at college, while driving back and forth to Montana to work or visit, the last one hundred miles of travel was generally conducted with the window down and my head cocked into the wind to smell my home coming.

So no, I don't blame our urban cousins for falling in love. How can they not? As it is an environment that I deeply cherish, so it can be for them as well. Indeed, so enchanted are some by the places that they are visiting, they have taken seriously the labeling that rural people often assign to their home regions. They call where we live the 'Last Best Places.' There is even a table top book that printed in 1992 entitled 'Montana: The Last

Best Place.' I most heartily concur.

Yet our urban visitors fall in love with more than just the scenery and the wildlife. They often fall in love with the rural culture with which they commune as they drive through. What they see often harkens to a different time in their nation. It can reflect some of the cultural norms that, along with the natural environment, many visitors had thought were long gone and only available through the lens of a Hollywood movie set.

What they witness is a slice of Americana that, in many ways, reflects what they perceive to be the fundamental traits of being 'American.' Inhabiting our resource-based communities are hardworking, hard-playing, family-oriented, community-oriented, school-oriented and church-oriented citizens that smack of a romanticized version of days gone by. So enthralled are they by some of the more romantic notions of the American west that I swear a cowboy riding beside one of the few interstates in Montana could cause a visitor to slide to a screeching stop and proclaim: 'Look, honey, a COWBOY!' Little do they know what that cowboy actually does, but there he is, and they fall in love with the hat and the belt buckle.

Visitors to our rural areas have no idea what makes our culture work. The same can be said for us in rural America. We don't know much about their urban lives. But they often like what they see in us. They may not like to live where we live, but they like that this fabric of the American cloth is still here. Many would be surprised to learn a few things about our culture, such as the fact that most of us have electricity – all the way to our houses! We have or are soon to get high speed internet. With our satellite dish, we get the same channels and watch the same news, sports and entertaining television shows they do. But we look different. Our setting is different. And they are rightfully intrigued.

When it is time to end their vacation and leave our rural areas to return to their homes in the city, many leave with a desire that rural people can and should understand and respect. They have a desire to protect those amazing Last Best Places they just visited. Some just want to know that the places they visited and fell in love with will remain culturally healthy and environmentally secure, even if they never get to come back. They assign a value to the fact that these rural areas 'exist.' Others want the areas they have visited to be protected so they can be assured that when they return for another visit it will remain the same. And a few leave with such a deep affinity for the rural areas that they may one day want to return to buy a ten or twenty-acre piece of that mecca. They may choose to permanently relocate or retire to the area, and as such they would like the place to be healthy if and when they get that chance.

Whatever the underlying reasoning, I understand and share our urban peers' desire to protect. I also understand that this desire provides the impetus for the efforts being made to protect, the ones that are pursued through legislative activism, regulatory activism and judicial activism. Unfortunately, this driving desire is oftentimes driving policy that has nothing to do with real protection of the environment and culture of the very places and things the public wants to protect.

Handling the nuances and insides and outs of a rural, resource-based economy and culture is not simple. Protecting the environment in the most sensible way possible is not simple. Yet often armed with little information or knowledge about the environmental, economic and social structures of rural areas, the policies clamored for have perverse impacts on both the environment and the communities of rural America.

Sadly, in case after case, the public's vision for the Last Best Places has one fatal flaw: there is no provision in it for the Last Best People living in these places. This is not because our urban cousins are ill-willed, mean-spirited or stupid. They are a very intelligent and rightfully concerned public who just wants policies in place to save the natural and cultural environment of our treasured rural landscape. But without a real world backdrop to their esoteric desires, many rural landscapes and communities are being protected…to death.

In this and every other nation in the industrialized world, policy is not driven by reality. Policy is driven by the public's perception of reality. When it comes to the public's perception of our rural environmental and cultural realities, Will Rogers was right. He once said, "It ain't what we don't know that gives us trouble, it's what we know that just ain't so." That statement is so tragically true, and the public knows a lot that 'just ain't so' about the Last Best Places that they want to protect.

Not only can we change this, we must. There is hope for understanding and, while we can never expect to agree on all things, we can still work together towards meaningful progress.

Part Three

Towards Progress

Chapter 14: The Timber Wars

In the 1980s and 90s, loggers and conservationists squared off on opposite sides of the "Timber Wars," as the media aptly dubbed it. Conflict erupted across the Pacific Northwest between certain environmental groups and loggers. It was a long, bitter and drawn-out battle over the future of our forest management. I was front row, center, for the whole thing.

In February of 1988, the United States Forest Service (USFS) asked me to help plan the annual contractors meeting for our area. They asked what I wanted on the agenda, usually things like changes to federal contracting and bonding requirements. But I told the forest supervisor that *before* we argue about changes in possible contracts, we best put something in place to make sure we had contracts to argue over.

By then, litigation was already out of control. Appeals by environmental groups were in place for any and all action proposed by the USFS. Scientists had begun to worry that species like the northern spotted owl and some salmon were headed for extinction due to a loss of habitat. As such, groups claiming to represent the interests of the public were dead set on stopping all logging on lands under public management. They were set on doing it through the courts.

In March and April of 1988, we held a series of meetings with loggers, mill workers and community leaders in northwestern Montana and northern Idaho. At the first meeting in Libby, some 275 loggers showed up. They were prepared for a dull day of hashing over the small print of federal contracts. Instead, I shared with them what we had learned about a recent Montana Wilderness Association seminar.

This association had become experts in using a well-intentioned forest management tool, covered briefly in Chapter Five, which paralyzed the USFS and halted forest management planning: the appeals process. The appeals process was built into the National Forest Management Act and is designed to give the public a voice in forest management discussions. Any of the 300 million Americans who had a concern over an action proposed by the USFS could send a letter of concern (an appeal) to the governing agency and demand answers to their questions before the proposed action could take place. The USFS must answer each of those concerns in a manner that satisfies the appellant before they can proceed with their action. This public engagement provision was put in place so that folks that are truly impacted by a proposed action (for example, the neighbor of USFS lands might be concerned about harvesting impacting their view or watershed) would have the ability to interact with, and presumably get satisfaction from, the federal agency prior to an action taking place.

The Montana Wilderness Association decided to use the appeals process to stop timber harvesting planned by the USFS in Montana. They convened a seminar at the University of Montana and taught more than 60 people in attendance how to use the appeals process to halt projects. One of the people who attended the gathering was a forester from Darby Lumber Company, some 350 miles south of Libby. The family who owned the mill was pretty dependent on timber supply from the national forests in their region and, with appeals of USFS management being used to stop harvesting in their area, the sawmill was running out of raw logs to process.

The Darby Lumber forester, Bill Crapser, was shocked at what he heard at the seminar. He gathered the written material from the meeting and shared it with me when he returned. The organizers instructed the participants to file appeals on anything and everything the USFS was doing. They stated that the important thing was the volume of appeals, not the veracity of the claims made in the appeals, and assured attendants that if they flooded the agency with masses of appeals the agency would be paralyzed. They wouldn't be able to function and so they wouldn't be able to move forward on timber management programming.

Included in the instructions for how to file an appeal were suggestions that appellants "be exhaustive, imaginative, nit-picky and philosophical in coming up with arguments. The good ones will score, the bad ones will just get shot down." Further, they said that they should, "never offer or consider any compromise on their demands," and that any action taken by the USFS that does not conform to our demands must be conformed to meet our demands or it must be stopped.

Much to Bill Crapser's dismay, they concluded the meeting by predicting that within one year they could halt USFS management in Montana and that within three years the paralysis within the agency would kill the sawmills in Montana. Bill was very, very afraid that they could achieve their goal, and left with a heavy heart. His attendance had modified some of the dialogue at the meeting, though. When they decided to do a round robin introduction in the room, the attendees each proudly stated their name, their national forest of interest and how many timber management plans they had personally halted. When the round robin reached Bill, he stated he was a forester and was a log purchaser for a small family sawmill that employed 100 families. According to Bill, that quieted the rhetoric of some in the room.

After sharing this experience with the loggers in attendance at the Libby meeting, I reminded them of what we had heard from Michael Scott from the Wilderness Society at our Montana Logging Association Annual meeting and his claim that we were 'visible and easy.' We could do little about being visible, but could quit being easy by making sure our voices were heard in the discussion of the disposition of the forests around our communities. We could stand together with a common voice and speak to what we knew to be true on the ground.

Some were thinking I was blowing the situation all out of proportion. They patiently put up with my cajoling. Others knew of the movement that was gaining steam and threatened our way of life. They were happy that we were at least talking about the issue. Nearly to a person, however, they were each fiercely independent businessmen and women who prided themselves in their personal can-do, standalone work ethic. Most had spent years in sometimes bitter competition with each other for the contracts offered by the USFS. They had a deep love of the isolationist type of work performed on their own in the woods, where their personal safety and their personal financial well-being was dictated not by others but by their ability to work hard and work smart. They were much more accustomed to fighting *with* each other than fighting *for* each other, but as the Timber Wars began, they learned that their survival dictated standing arm and arm with their peers (even if those peers were previously their adversaries).

And so it started. I visited nearly a dozen small logging towns in northern Idaho and western Montana. On April 15th, over 3,500 people gathered in Libby at our first big community rally. We were able to gain the attention of lots of regional print, radio and television media. Since cameras were showing up along with the throngs of voters, we were able to convince two US senators and two US representatives to attend as well. We were becoming 'news.'

On May 3rd, at a meeting in Eureka, Montana, log trucker Mike Mrgich suggested we haul logs to Darby Lumber, the mill where forester Bill Crapser worked, in Darby, Montana. The mill had announced that day they were closing their doors because of massive appeals against the USFS. When I brought the idea to a Vincent Logging meeting, my brother Will suggested if we were going to haul logs to a mill to keep it open, we had better plan on hauling a lot of logs. On May 13th, 303 loaded trucks from five western states delivered over a million board feet to the Darby Mill in what became known as the Great Northwest Log Haul. *NBC News* covered the event live on their evening news. That night, after the rally, we started a grassroots group called Communities for a Great Northwest and set a goal to activate forest communities throughout the Pacific Northwest. Monday morning, 100 employees of Darby Lumber went to work instead of the unemployment line.

When *NBC News* aired our 'convoy' and rally, phone calls began to come into the Vincent Logging office from all over the country. The first call I got was from Corydon, Indiana. The Hoosier National Forest had been shut down by appeals and wilderness debates. Local forest workers in that area wanted to know what they could do to help us help them. Then called farmers, ranchers, miners and fisherman. They shared their fear of being socially and politically engineered off of the land and out of the ocean. Calls came from Arizona, California, Illinois, Florida, Texas, Oregon, Idaho, upstate New York and northern Michigan. Sometimes it felt like rural America was under siege.

Three months later, over 1,200 logging trucks and countless community support vehicles formed a multi-state convoy to Grants Pass to what was called the Silver Fire Roundup. At the fairgrounds in Grants Pass, the cavalcade had to pass a throng of Earth First! protesters who had gathered at the front gate. They had signs calling us murderers of the forest and killers of the planet.

When all of the vehicles had been parked and the participants assembled, there was a crowd of over 10,000 in the stands. Jim Petersen, executive director of the Evergreen Foundation and organizer of the event, asked me to say a few words. I was, once more, scared to death. In front of me was the biggest crowd I had addressed since my college days. And these weren't students!

I took a deep breath, tried to keep the bile in the back of my throat from erupting and grabbed the mic. My heart was pounding as I looked into the stands... and I saw 20,000 tired eyes filled with a mixture of concern, anxiety, fear and an inkling of hope staring back at me. Like a knife stabbing through my chest, I suddenly realized these people had heard, at some time in their lives, the same message shared with my folks in our little rural school in Libby, the message that 'they did not have a heritage worthy of passing on.' Somewhere inside them was the lingering question of whether or not they and their culture had a place in our modern world. I could see the mantles of guilt worn across those stands.

A quietness had come over the crowd as they waited for me to say something. Instead of giving my prepared remarks, I veered and softly said, "It's okay to be a logger." You'd have thought I asked them to please tear the grandstands down. They began to stand and cheer and clap and scream at the tops of their lungs. It was almost as if they were, in unison, ripping off their own individuals mantles and flinging them into the air. They did not want to stop. They were not done. It went on for nearly five minutes.

For the next several years we worked hard on raising awareness. From 1988 through 1992, community meetings, rallies and convoys were almost weekly events. They were held in all of the western states. We convoyed to places like Missoula, Montana, Forks, Washington and Susanville, California. We rallied in towns and cities such as Olympia and Omak, Washington, Yreka and Eureka, California, Phoenix and Sedona, Arizona and Sweethome and Salem, Oregon. Some 500 people met in a gymnasium in Philomath, Oregon. 5,000 ranchers and loggers gathered in Missoula. 7,500 people met in Pioneer Park in Olympia. 15,000 people gathered in Pioneer Park in downtown Portland.

We began to form coalitions of loggers, ranchers, farmers and fisherman who were all feeling the pressures of being 'saved to death.' Grassroots groups popped up in nearly every town in the west with names like Communities for a Greater Oregon, the Oregon Lands Coalition, People for the West, Montanans for Multiple Use. There were, literally, hundreds of community organizing groups that formed during these years.

We also began to form a cadre of outstanding community leaders who gave of their time, energy and money to help with the effort. Some were long-time rural advocates like firebrands Chuck Cushman and Ron Arnold from Washington and Perry Pendley of Mountain States Legal Foundation in Denver. Most were new leaders (like myself) and some came from Libby, such as my high school friend and neighbor Ed Eggleston and my friends Connie Wood, Chuck and Charlotte Woods and Dan and Colleen Snyder. Others from Montana included Webb Brown, Peggy Wagner, Kathy Bennedetto and my current business partner in Environomics, Tammy Johnson. Leaders from the west included Valerie Johnson, Tom Hirons, Jim Petersen, Iris Butler and a plethora of others from Oregon as well as Nadine Bailey, Liz Smith, Rose Comstock and Donn Zea from California. Rita Carlson was from Idaho, Larry Mason and Collin King led from Forks, Washington. In the east came Elizabeth Pease of Tennessee, Harry and Doris MacIntosh from New York and Brian Bishop from Rhode Island. These are just a few of the many, many folks who put enormous amounts of their personal time, energy and money into awareness-raising efforts. Some have become lifelong friends. Others hold a special place in my heart that is cordoned off for those who gave freely of themselves for our fight.

When we formed a national group, the Alliance for America, we had an annual national budget of under $50,000. Individually and collectively our groups and coalitions had precious little monetary resources, even though the anti-logging forces claimed we were nothing but 'industry front' groups rolling in cash. Our lack of money was more than compensated for with our enthusiasm and determination. We continued making the clamor we believed was moving us towards a rightful resolution. Some of our gatherings were huge and garnered national attention. All of our gatherings were designed to gain media coverage in order to raise both the public's and our elected leaders' awareness of the issues our rural communities faced.

In these early days, those leading the timber community side of the unfolding war thought all we needed was to get the attention of our elected leaders, 'educate' them and the public about the 'truth' of American forest management and, like magic, corrective action would be taken to fix our problems. It was a simple formula: raise awareness, educate the masses and the leaders – and poof! – a solution would appear. Then we could go back to work.

We were so, so dreadfully wrong.

We had succeeded in getting the nation's attention. The Timber Wars were now raging on the national stage. But we were nowhere near reaching a resolution that would let us go back to work. The front lines of the Timber Wars included two different sets of encamped and embattled strident supporters. While I helped lead the news-making rallies, convoys and marches on capital buildings, the Sierra Club and others began a 'Zero Cut' campaign to halt all logging on public lands, while the Earth First! contingent was busy practicing their eco-terror brand of warfare that destroyed hundreds of millions of dollars of logging equipment.

The Audubon Society even got in on the fun. They sent a reporter to Montana to interview me about the budding Timber Wars and the growing grassroots movement in the rural west. I was excited to have them come to town and do a story. The Audubon reporter, John G. Mitchell, interviewed me and spent several weeks following me around the northwest as we held community meetings, rallies and convoys.

He ultimately authored a several part series printed in *Audubon Magazine* about our efforts. It was simply astonishing, for lack of a better word. In his piece, he called me the 'John the Baptist' of the Timber Town rebellion, claimed that I was 'chosen' as a young child by Plum Creek Timber Company (you can't make this stuff up…) and put through college by that company and then positioned in Libby, Montana, to organize a movement that would allow them to rape and pillage the public's forests. He made some disparaging comments about the forlorn look in my brown eyes as I traveled the countryside convening mountaintop hideaway brainwashing sessions for up-and-coming rural rabble rousers (my eyes are bluish green, and I assure you he saw them up close). It didn't matter, I guess. His story claimed that I was impregnating the brains of the poor rural folks with messages developed in focus groups convened by Plum Creek public relations specialist. Apparently, unbeknownst to me, I had assisted in crafting a whole new language that was bastardizing the true meaning of conservation and stewardship. It was a great story, truly an epic work of fiction.

And so, the war raged on. We did have some early wins in our effort to save our timber towns and families. Our wins, however, were few and far between. The national forest timber program was collapsing. The Ninth Circuit Court of Appeals was hearing cases brought forward by the environmental conflict industry and issued ruling after ruling that slammed the door on the face of our rural timber towns. Sawmills were closing, loggers were forced out of business, main streets of our small towns were barely hanging on, our school funding systems were failing and the American public did not seem to care.

We also tried to use the courts. William Perry Pendley of the Mountain States Legal Foundation represented Lincoln County, Montana, in a suit against the USFS for 'failure to manage for a healthy forest.' The county was the first in the nation to gain standing in a forest lawsuit. We won the argument that without management our forests were going to burn to the ground, but we lost the case as the federal judge ruled that our remedy (marginally increased logging) was not sufficient enough to negate the certain loss of our forests to fires.

We had high hopes that when newly-elected President Clinton agreed to convene a 'Timber Summit,' we could get to the bottom of our issue. We organized a gathering of some 15,000 people in Portland, Oregon, and held rallies during the two-day Summit. While our rally and the President's summit made a great deal of news, it accomplished nothing in the real world of forest management. Our families, our towns and our forests were still under siege and we were losing the war.

The Timber Wars consumed the energy, resources and human talent of a lot of us in the rural west, but we were fighting the good fight. Or so we thought.

———

Chapter 15: Looking in the Mirror

In those tumultuous days of the Timber Wars, we perfected the art of fighting. We wore ourselves down pitching battles against policy and court decisions. We knew the public's forested lands were going to be imperiled by management regimes dictated by bureaucrats and judges who neither lived in nor understood the economic, social and environmental nuances.

Over time, a feeling of helplessness began to wash over me and other grassroots activists. Our timber towns were collapsing. Our businesses were failing. Timber workers were being laid off by the tens of thousands. Our forests were being managed into cinders by the scientifically predicted and catastrophically huge, catastrophically hot forest fires driven by mismanagement and overstocking. We were losing.

Standing among the ruins, it was time to really take stock. We looked at where we had been, where we were and where we wanted to go. We took a long look in the mirror.

What we had done wrong? What had we done right? And what we must do to ultimately 'save' our forests and our forest communities?

The mirror was not a fun thing to stare at. It gave us some chilling glimpses of truths we had long ignored.

What were we doing that was wrong? Why wasn't it working? We certainly were not winning in the court of public opinion. This confused us. We were right. The anti-logging fanatics were wrong. Of that we were sure.

We were so sure about our righteous mission that we failed to do some of the things that would open the public's minds to us and our arguments. We failed to listen. We failed to empathize with them and understand their concerns. We failed to display the needed level of tolerance and understanding of views that did not match what we believed so wholeheartedly to be true.

We were angry and we acted like it. We were angered when anti-logging interests would treat us like uneducated knuckle-draggers. Too often we responded to them with blanket generalizations of condemnation. We were incensed the public just did not understand we were the true environmentalists. After all, we worked in and loved the environment they so badly wanted to protect! Our futures were interwoven with the long-term health of the forest they claimed we were destroying.

Our claim to being the true environmentalists must have sounded fairly hollow to the public. Particularly when we sometimes made disparaging remarks in anger about 'those damn stupid environmentalists.' The language we used in framing the enemy position sure sounded good in the heat of battle. But it also served as a constant reminder that we were not in sync with the majority of Americans who considered themselves 'environmentally' aware.

Our demands that the public empathize with the people, institutions, values and opinions of our culture was not matched by a similar show of empathy for the urban people, institutions, values and opinions. Before we ever got to discuss our issues, we clearly indicated to the 80 percent of Americans who live in urban areas we were not like them. We wanted the public to understand we were the caretakers of the environment while at the same time using disparaging language that attempted to discredit those 'bastards' the public assumed were watching out for the public's interest in the environment.

We (and by that I refer to myself) also suffered from a tendency to use our mouths way more than we used our ears. We had neglected to do one incredibly important thing concerning the public: listen. We needed to hear what the public was saying and begin to understand how the public was coming to the conclusions they reached on the issues impacting our interests.

Listening to people who are armed with a lifetime of disinformation, misinformation, half-truths and outright lies is not easy. But the ugly truth we had to address was that they were thinking the same about us. For too long, rural people, myself included, joked about public ignorance with refrains such as: 'those silly people from the city think milk comes from a carton at Safeway... chuckle, chuckle.' 'Those stupid people in Seattle think boards just show up at Home Depot... chuckle, chuckle.'

We often felt a bit self-righteous about what we knew and what they didn't know. Why? Because lurking in the backs of our minds was the niggling feeling that we don't have many legs up on our urban cousins, but we dang well know where their stuff comes from. These seemingly innocent jokes weren't, and still aren't, funny. Interestingly, and perhaps sadly, they continue to be told.

We needed to not only have listened to what the public was saying so we could better engage with them in a real discussion, but we also needed to do what we were asking of them: put ourselves in their shoes. We ought to have walked a mile in the shoes of the non-natural resource embedded public.

The public, though possibly ill-informed, is not stupid. They are rightfully concerned about the environment. They are also three (or four) generations removed from the farm, have no direct natural resource linkage and are trying to make difficult choices about complex environmental issues.

We took a hard look at their conclusions and the choices they seemed dead set on making, choices that impacted our lives and our forests. We asked one simple question: what would we do if we were them? What would we base our conclusions on if we lived in New York or Los Angeles?

Most of the population does not have a lifetime of ground-based reality upon which to rely when discerning the ins and outs of the natural world. They have a lifetime of *National Geographic* documentaries at best and Disney movies at worst. These sanitized and dramatized versions of the world we live in has helped shape the worldview of the vast majority of our industrialized society.

For most, visons of pre-human earth elicit images of global harmony and balance, where butterflies flit in beautiful green fields or wolves raise orphaned rabbits. This Disneyesque Ecotopia has been woven into the foundational plots of hundreds of movies. *We* know that in the real world wolves eat the rabbits (orphaned or not), and there is no forest-wide party right after the last bone is crushed and swallowed. But the disconnected public knows little of nature's harsh realities.

The evildoer of choice in most movies: humans. The message is not subtle. Movies are merely entertainment and not meant to reflect reality, but I can assure you that fifty years of *Bambi* has had an effect on how the public has come to understand the human relationship with 'nature.' Movies like *Fern Gully*, *Hoot*, *Avatar*, *Free Willy* and others have a common theme: capitalism destroys the environment and good people must fight it.

Humanizing nature and vilifying humans sells movie tickets and children's books. But it also creates fertile ground for fear-mongering marketing campaign. It sets the stage for a problem in dealing with real environmental issues.

Economy and ecology come from the same Greek root: *oikos* or eco. *Oikos* means 'house.' The outside of our house, our ecology, is joined at the hip with the inside of our house, or our economy. Action in our ecology will have a direct impact on our economy and vise-versa. If we do not have a healthy environment we cannot hope to build and sustain a healthy economy. If we do not have a healthy economy, we cannot expect to have the economic luxury of caring appropriately for the environment.

The debate over the environment that is raging in the industrialized world is possible because we have societies with the economic luxury of debate. People in poverty do not have long and serious discussions about 'viewsheds' or 'scenic vistas' until after they figure out what they are going to do to get dinner on the plates of their children. The environment takes a back seat until basic needs are met through some sort of profit-centered economy.

This isn't commonly discussed in public debate. It's not something people think about. And our early years of yelling at them with our 'truths' did not move them toward a greater understanding but, rather, firmed up their opposition to our position in the debate. In hindsight, who could blame them? We were, to them, 'destroying the earth' and had the gall to demand that they give us their blessing to continue committing our atrocities against nature.

In today's soundbite society, people are given easily digestible snippets of information about environmental policy. Our complex forestry issue has, for decades, been boiled down into two twenty-second soundbites with stock photos or B-roll for a visual backdrop. It's 'pro-logging' interests or 'save-the-forest' interests. The backdrop used for the 'industry' position invariably shows the world's largest clear cut (you can see that sucker from the moon) with the very last tree tottering over to join a sea of dead stumps. The person on screen is either a knuckle-dragging Neanderthal with chewing tobacco dribbling down his chin and an 'eat-an-owl' t-shirt proclaiming that 'God I like to make stumps,' or a three-piece suit-and-tie talking head from a multinational timber company saying 'America wants wood products and by God we provide them.'

The next twenty-second visual is a babbling brook with a pristine mountain scene full of lovely trees. An earnest young man or women proclaims their simple desire to protect the forest for future generations from the greedy corporate bastards who want to cut down all of the world's trees.

Resource industry issues have long suffered from this type

of framing. News stories about mining show first a yellow river flowing from a poisoned settling pond with dead birds followed by twenty seconds of an earnest millennial who simply wants clean air and water. Stories on modern farming show silt and chemicals running off of a field into an algae-choked stream followed by a person on the banks of the little Bitterroot River asking for nothing more than safe water and food for our children. Animal agriculture stories have, for several years, used a sad video clip of some dairy farmer in California sticking a forklift tine through a black-and-white spotted cow, dragging it through six inches of runny manure to a death pile of carcasses, while the anti-animal agriculture spokesperson holds and pets a puppy begging through tears for nothing more than humane care of our farm animals.

When we rural people see our issues boiled down to the two choices of 'preserve and protect' or 'destroy with the human hand,' we get angry. And in the early days of the Timber Wars, we let these types of portrayals of who we are, and what we do, fuel the anger we needed to continue fighting for Our Truths.

But again, back to the mirror. When we finally looked into it, we understood that we needed to ask ourselves that same simple question: If we were the public and had an interest in the environment, but had no resource background other than a lifetime of Disney movies under our belt, which of the two choices being presented would get our support? The answer was disconcerting. If we had one functioning brain cell the choice would be incredibly easy. We would not choose to have our forests all cut down. We would not choose to have our rivers running yellow with mining wastes. We would not choose to poison our waters or our foods with chemicals. We would not endorse punching through the sides of poor old cows with a forklift.

The public, we finally determined, is doing just what we would do if we had no understanding of the many choices of conservation and stewardship that lie between the two choices presented to them. Recognizing this reality was incredibly important because it illuminated the real problem: ignorance.

The ignorance we needed to address was not just on the part of the uninformed public, it included our own ignorance. There's a difference between fighting over the direction of bad environmental policy, and leading a discussion that could yield a correction in bad policy.

Addressing the public's ignorance over forest management and our ignorance in leading the discussion was not as easy as holding rallies and convoys and shouting our truths from street corners. It was not as easy as identifying the environmental conflict industry as villains and inventing or capitalizing on real or perceived environmental crises and using them to drum up the emotion that fueled our battles. We knew, though, that what we had been doing was incredibly counterproductive in the long run. In fact, we seemed to be the perfect foil central to the long-term strategic business plans of the conflict industry we so despised. We were, I am afraid, the third ring of a three-ring circus and they were the ones taking the gate receipts.

The eco-conflict industry had developed an outstanding business strategy in which we were unknowingly participating. The public's concern about the environment and lack of real information on the subject provided fertile ground for their marketing plans. All that they needed was their own villain - us. Do you want the marching Neanderthals to whack all of the trees down or do you want to help to 'save the forest' by sending our non-governmental organizations (NGOs) some desperately needed cash?'

We helped them raise billions of dollars.

It was time to end the Timber Wars. It was time to begin crafting solutions we could live with and that would protect both our forests and our forest-dependent culture. It was the more difficult task, and we had to bust many of our myths along the way.

Myth: Crazy Can't Happen Here

When the issues about forest management first heated up, we thought that the urbanites from the 'left' coast were driving the insanity we were watching, and that insanity would not find a home in places like Montana. We were commonsense folk and common sense would win in the end.

Fact: Crazy is Portable

People may not recognize our version of 'common sense.' They (like us) recognize their own version that is crafted out of their personal beliefs and realities. They will fight for their long-held beliefs because (also like us) they think they are right – and we are wrong.

Myth: It's a Pendulum Thing

Many of us, myself included, thought that the whole environmental issue was being taken to the extreme by some zealots, but that social movements often swing past the 'middle' ground before they begin to correct and 'swing' back. In time, the public will realize that they had been taken for a ride and will react with moderation.

Fact: It's NOT a Pendulum Thing

The issue of the environment is not a 'pendulum' thing. Society is rightfully concerned about their environment and are trying to make difficult moral and ethical decisions on a whole range of complex ecological issues. When this rightfully concerned society seeks a compromise or a 'middle ground' solution and base their conclusions on information that is not accurate, then the supposed 'middle ground' is nowhere near the 'middle' that makes sense to those living in the impact zone.

Myth: The Truth Will Win

We were positive that the truth about America's forests

would win the day. We hit the streets armed with a plethora of Truths: the timber industry plants six trees for each tree harvested; there is more forested land in America today than there was 100 years ago; our management methods promote sustainable forest growth because our future depends upon those growing forests; if we don't manage the forest then nature will burn them in catastrophically huge and hot fires; biodiversity is enhanced when we manage the forest correctly.

We were absolutely positive that our truths were grounded in reality and that when we shared them with the public they would see the light. Our light. We laughed out loud at the public when we learned how little they knew about their forests and about the people who work in the forest. 'Those silly people in Seattle.' We knew we were smart and the public was stupid when it came to understanding the forest environment.

Fact: We Were Playing Reverse Jeopardy

A term embraced by my friend Eric Williams, who works in the public relations industry, is 'reverse jeopardy.' It's a sad game I participated in for nearly a decade. We compiled talking points and fact sheets and had armed our warriors with The Truth. One day during the heat of battle, Eric pointed out to me a startling fact. We were answering all of the questions the public wasn't asking. We were so busy shouting at the public we didn't have time or desire to listen to what they were telling us they wanted to know. We knew that the public just needed our set of truths and we were determined to cram those truths down their stupid throats.

A classic example of this was the timber industry's 'Wood Is Good' campaign. During the height of the

Timber Wars, the industry called in a public relations specialist from Europe. The specialist told industry executives to remove all reference to logging and harvesting from promotional materials. Instead, he said, we should focus on the finished wood products and highlight a female consumer enjoying our wood products in order to promote Mother Earth. The industry obliged and ran a $40-million-dollar advertising campaign that specifically avoided discussing forest management. We also beat up on our potential allies when the same advertising campaign championed wood as good and steel, aluminum and concrete as 'bad.'

The public, however, was already convinced that wood is good. They were enjoying a record consumption of our products. In other words, the public loved our finished wood product but maintained a firmly held belief that 'stumps suck' and our multi-million-dollar tone-deaf advertising campaign was an expensive exercise in reverse jeopardy. We ignored the questions the public had about harvesting, and left that entire discussion up to those who did not like our practices – like the Sierra Club. These groups were not tone-deaf, did not play reverse jeopardy, listened to what the public was concerned about and maximized the profit-making potential of that concern. Meanwhile, we had pretty women pointing at wooden doors and windows.

We finally learned that 'truth' is a nebulous term that is, much like common sense, crafted out of personal beliefs, worldview, realities and information sources. We did not make a dent in the public's firmly held beliefs about forests and forest management until we finally put our bullhorns down, listened to what the public was saying, listened to what their concerns were and started crafting answers to their questions in language they could understand and accept.

Chapter 16: You Don't Need Consensus for Progress

There's one really easy way to get others to agree with you and see things your way. In fact, it's no challenge at all to get them to corroborate your views and support your causes. How do you do this? Simple. Only talk to those who already hold the same beliefs as you!

As we learned the hard way in the Timber Wars, when it comes down to it, we seldom even try to communicate with those holding opposing views, dissenting beliefs or different visions of what is right or good. And even more rare is trying to truly understand and grasp the significance, importance or implications of what was communicated. Being honest, how often do we communicate with "the other side" in order to exchange ideas or build understanding? Most of the time we just want to explain to them why we are correct, why they are incorrect, or both.

Communicating and understanding is hard. We frequently disparage people for going overboard on 'political correctness.' However, what if two parties come together for the purpose of communicating their stances on sensitive topics? There's the very real possibility that an insensitive slip of the tongue by one side permanently severs the lines of communication.

The need for carefully chosen words so as not to offend the opposing party, even if their views and beliefs differ significantly, is criticized in popular media today. But we would do well to remember that insults, hurt feelings, an undying commitment to being right and the sense that we don't need to care about anyone else's view has resulted in the very situation we faced.

"Well, if we could ever get the crazies to listen." Or, "You know those nut-jobs." Or, "You need to explain it to those morons who think that ..." We shouldn't be surprised that when we use such language to describe other human beings, those other human beings do not feel any increased desire to understand our point of view. Stated bluntly, what did you expect?

History has shown us few cases of people understanding and respecting dissenting views without seeking to change the opposing party or "win" somehow. Yet do any of us, any single one of us, enjoy being forcibly convinced of a viewpoint that we don't agree with? That's not a conversation anyone wants to participate in, because it's not really a conversation.

The lack of productive conversation is usually acknowledged by both parties. If there's no agreement to be had, why should I make the effort? A person shows up ready to defend, if they even show up at all. So where does the failure to communicate and understand come from? Is it because it's actually unlikely? Or is it because we've already discounted a chance for real communication because we *know*, before even giving the other side a shot, that we will refuse to change our own position?

So then we show up for the spectators. We show up ready to convince the spectators that we are *right*, and the other side is *wrong*. Or perhaps that they are incorrect, misguided or downright evil. It depends on the situation, right? Choose your label.

Given the broad audiences that exist on social media, and

how easy it is to communicate to large audiences through such channels, under the guise of a 'discussion' two opposing parties' communication devolves into a spectator sport in which both parties try to "win supporters" at the expense of the other side. There's no real exchange of ideas or viewpoints taking place. Perhaps some points are made here or there, but there's little potential for progress. Understanding the views of others, particularly those in sharp dissention, does not happen by accident or as a byproduct.

All the communication in the world won't mean anything, however, if it is blocked by intolerance. If a person is unwilling to accept someone else's views, beliefs or behaviors simply because they are different form his or her own - it's just intolerance. But intolerance is generally the second barrier, because to get there, you have to be communicating with one another to begin with (not *at* one another). Yet if upon becoming aware of a person's dissenting views you choose to ignore them, discount them or find ways to convince yourself that they're 'wrong'? Again, it's just intolerance.

An unwillingness to accept different views is sometimes seen as a natural extension of our human desire to protect ourselves, and our desire to protect our view of ourselves. But we need to get over that. Refusing to accept dissenting views creates barriers. It just resets the cycle: lack of communication, intolerance, refusal to accept. Are we so fragile that we must protect our sense of self so vigilantly that we can't even attempt to understand why someone else feels a certain way?

When we set out to talk to someone on the other side of an emotionally charged issue, especially one that challenges a closely held moral or ethical beliefs, chances are high the conversation will end with two disagreeing parties. Even if the intention of the exchange is to explain and willingly attempt to understand what is being communicated in return, the other party may not change their views dramatically. There's no guarantee that just because someone listens and understands you, they will take to your side.

Say there's a group that believes that the waters running

through a specific river tributary need to remain untouched and protected from any human intervention. Another group believes the waterway should be diverted for the building of an energy generating dam. Those opposing the project feel the waterway is so beautiful and pristine, destruction would violate their basic principles as stewards of the land. And if it's someone's hometown park or nearby favorite hiking trail, the place where they hiked and fished with their now deceased grandfather, the disagreement over altering that waterway may be so emotionally charged that no amount of sharing dissenting opinions would alter their stance. Or maybe even the waterway is particularly important to a specific species of fish, and if someone were so committed towards the survival of all species in the area, then perhaps no amount of discussion or sharing of dissenting views would alter their stance.

So what's the point then? Well, lack of progress is often blamed on the inability to convince someone else that you're 'right.' But consider the potential for progress even if there is disagreement. **Progress does not require consensus**. We don't have to all agree with each other on everything. We won't, anyway. That's unrealistic because we're all different, with different life experiences and backgrounds and principles. But we *do* have to be willing to understand and accept the views of others, even if we don't agree. That means beating back the real enemies: ignorance, intolerance and an unwillingness to accept different views. It doesn't mean changing our minds, ditching our morals or agreeing with everyone.

Self-verification and self-policing have become the cornerstone of many industries' attempts to quiet fears, or at least begin to respond to concerns, of the public. These issues can range from labor disputes and worker treatment to environmental degradation. Many support the argument, "who better to verify that things are being done to the 'correct standard' than those most familiar with the industry?"

Well, the "correct standard" is usually up for debate. Those involved in production tend to have different views than those involved in the consumption. There is much ongoing work in this regard, such as the perception of beef cattle systems by 'consumers versus producers' by Dr. Glynn Tonsor at Kansas State University and similar assessments on dairy cattle production systems by Dr. Christopher Wolf at Michigan State University. Researchers also look at the differences in view or vision of the "correct standard" and how elusive this can be. Ongoing work from prominent agricultural economists, including Drs. Jayson Lusk and Bailey Norwood at Oklahoma State University, look at just that.

In general, those working in production of a good or service report being less concerned about the production process than consumers of that good or service. The act of being involved in the production system makes them more aware, and more comfortable with, the practices used. If a producer was truly uncomfortable with a production system, it's generally thought they would either seek to alter it or no longer participate in production of that good or service.

If the policing and verifying is left to producers, the standards sought to be enforced or met are usually different than those that would have been preferred by the general public. Consumer-envisioned standards may well be harder to meet. After all, it would be counterintuitive to expect producers to always readily increase stringency. This usually also increases difficulty and cost, or at least adds to the record-keeping. So while producers may indeed be the most familiar and most knowledgeable, their standards might not match up with what the rest of the public wants.

The second question is if it is realistic to expect that those who stand to profit be the ones enforcing standards and regulations on *that very same* production system? Yes, those people directly involved have the most understanding of the processes and production. But there is an undeniable potential for some very perverse incentives.

For instance, would there be the incentive to turn in a "bad actor" who may not be following industry guidelines? In the case of a legal standard or regulation, there is government oversight. Government oversight ensures a backstop of sorts. It provides assurance to consumers and the public that someone without direct interest in the performance of a firm or industry is watching.

A lot of work has gone into determining who is the 'optimal verifier.' Given the variation in agricultural and natural resource products, from milk-based infant formula to wood furniture, it really depends. And given how differently the public perceives certain verifiers, different groups of people will tend to trust one over another, anyway. There are many factors to be considered, and trust is fluid. It can change over time, particularly in the face of a big failure.

Because of these challenges, many industry and producer groups have formed non-traditional partnerships with other organizations. For example, producer groups are investing in university research to figure out what groups of people want what types of characteristics and production processes. Research conducted within an industry itself isn't always convincing to the broader public. More than ever, traditional industries like agriculture and natural resource management are considering paying for outside, third-party research.

There are some organizations that exist solely to validate claims and perform surprise audits or checks on production. But in other cases, there have even been some unlikely partnerships formed between organizations who were once foes in the past. For example, livestock animal welfare claims may be validated by animal welfare consumer groups. The willingness by producers to have their standards validated by groups that serve as "industry watchdogs" serves to, in many cases, convince the public they are truly committed to doing the 'right thing.' Having validation from a 'foe' rather than a 'friend' sends the strongest message of compliance, because no one doubts or suspects there was any kind of incentive to overlook mistakes.

But forming relationships with former enemies can be tense if not downright ugly. For instance, asking a group to check your standards, if your standards are lower than what they want, may not go well. It only works if both parties agree to disagree, or agree to march forward towards a common goal without consensus on precisely what that common goal looks like.

This issue has been central to moving forward with stakeholder groups concerned about forest practices on public lands. We now have nearly twenty years of collaboration under our belts and are working together with forest health as our common goal. The definition of what is 'healthy' within a forest ecosystem yields hours and hours of vigorous discussion and airing of differences. This discussion and its vigor pales in comparison to the ensuing discussion and vigorous debate concerning the methodology and management techniques required to reach the hard-fought notion of a 'healthy' forest. We don't always agree, but we have learned that we can find enough common ground to move forward for the good of our forests and our forest communities.

It is difficult, but not impossible. In the case of the animal welfare group and livestock producers, both groups may agree on a set of standards, which improves animal welfare. The animal welfare organization may not be validating practices they believe are good enough. But they may validate the lesser standards anyway because to do so moves a portion of the industry voluntarily towards better animal welfare. The eventual goal remains elusive. And it's likely the two groups do not, and will not, agree on it. However, working together towards progress is possible without consensus, as long as you have tolerance and acceptance of differing beliefs or views.

Chapter 17: We're All Hypocrites

Everyone hates a hypocrite, right? And boy is hypocrisy easy to spot in others. It's even easier to call out. I've given in and taken the easy shot more times than I care to count. I've also learned that while it momentarily feels good to take the easy shot, that short-term endorphin release just isn't worth it. It puts the other person on the defensive and opens up the door for a free shot at me and *my* positions on a subject.

Years ago, I attended the wedding of a niece in Connecticut. A family member was waiting for me to arrive, and she could barely contain her glee at the opportunity to slay what she saw as my anti-environmental opinions. When we pulled up to my in-law's house, I spotted a bumper sticker on a 40-foot-long Winnebago with Ohio license plates. At the time, there was a national debate raging about drilling for oil in the Arctic National Wildlife Refuge (ANWR) area of Alaska. The 4 mile-per-gallon behemoth of a vehicle, which had just driven 500 miles, showcased a 'Save ANWR' bumper-sticker. I knew that the owner of said vehicle was the same relative awaiting my arrival in order to filet me and my resource background.

Sure enough, when I got inside, she was waiting and pounced. Luckily, this was near the end of the worst of the Timber Wars and I had learned a few things. First off, I knew that there are some people who will never move off their position of antagonism, no matter what evidence is shared. I also learned that I, too, had my own share of hypocrisy that could be thrown in my face. I am, after all, from a rural western state, one in which the citizens like to think we can get by just fine without the strong arm of the federal government dictating our lives, while being the fourth most dependent state on federal government support (according to Wallet Hub). Without the federal government, our infrastructure would be in big, big trouble. On top of that, I support regulated, modern mining and we also happen to live in a town that is a Super Fund Site due to the legacy of mining issues. So, yeah, we too are hypocrites.

Leaning on my hard lessons learned, rather than fling her hypocrisy in her face (the bumper sticker was really, really hard to not use as a battle cry), I listened. I learned a lot about how she came to believe what she believed. On the issue of forestry, I was able to have a discussion with her about forest health. The family put their popcorn away (they were ready to watch a fight), and I had a visit instead. I learned a bit more about the mindset of those who do not understand our issues, I didn't open myself up to the backlash of my own hypocrisy and I didn't put her on the immediate defensive.

*   *   *

Hypocrisy can be a serious communication barrier, one to which we all fall prey. Have you ever told someone, or even told yourself, one of the following? "I ran today, thus I can eat this *whole pizza.*" "I donated $X to a charitable cause, thus it is *okay* if I spend 6 times $X on frivolity." "I worked late last night, so it is *totally fine* if I goof off all day today." Or maybe even, "I went to the gym this morning after breakfast, so I *earned* this chocolate cake dessert after dinner." The last of which is an argument that may work (well, not really) if we all agree to pay no mind to the celebratory cupcake already consumed on the way home from the gym.

Isn't it true that we all tend to justify and even overstate our own goodness? For example, I ran five miles this morning, or I donated to charity, so I can now justify my 'less' good (or perhaps even *bad*) behaviors? These minor indulgences are perhaps not perfectly consistent with hypocrisy. Yet justifications skate dangerously close to the line. If not hypocritical, they are the justifications of one seeking to buy themselves out of their own guilt. I value health and well-being, now hand me the cake – but it's okay, because I did complete actions supporting my stated values before happy hour (or cake-o'clock).

Hypocritical behaviors are everywhere in the most mundane activities of our everyday life. The most relatable are those counter to our stated 'beliefs' regarding our personal actions, such as household spending or food and health. But people are particularly funny when it comes to pledging support for causes, and then adjusting, or *not* adjusting, one's behaviors to support such causes.

Actions that directly violate our stated priorities run rampant, and this is particularly true around matters of environmentalism. You could argue it's impossible to even live normally in some form of shelter with some form of energy for heat, light and/or transportation and *not* create negative impacts on the environment. Simply living could contradict a stated intention to care for and prioritize (or even want to *save*) the environment.

The argument frequently lofted at environmental activists, or those professing concern for climatic change, is their hypocrisy for daring to live and breathe (or live anything resembling a normal life in modern society). A person may have a very defined intention to protect the environment not just for him or herself, but for the children and grandchildren. Yet the need to commute to work and heat the home may cause negative impacts on that very same environment.

Complicating matters further, economic pressures can influence behavior. It often exacerbates the distance between beliefs and behavior. Take the environmentalist who needs shelter, heat and transportation. Perhaps he has two heat source options. Option One is relatively cheap, perhaps costing $X/month, but it comes with a cost to the environment. Option Two is relatively expensive, costing $4X/month, or four times as much as Option One. But it only causes 25 percent of the environmental damage.

Suppose our environmentalist cannot afford to pay for Option Two because he doesn't have enough money. Is he less of an environmentalist because he has pursued heat via an environmentally damaging path? Even though he is no less caring nor feels less of an ethical or moral obligation to protect it?

Consider another environmentalist. It is December in northern Montana, which means it is bitterly cold and heat isn't a luxury, it's a necessity. She *could* technically afford to pay for heat using Option Two, but goes for the cheaper option to save some money. Does it matter what she does with the money she saved by heating her home with the cheaper option? Would donating the money saved on heating to environmental causes make our environmentalist less of a hypocrite?

These environmentalist "hypocrites" reside in a society characterized by consumption. Modern economies today depend on consumption. If someone wants to improve the economy, they likely seek to encourage consumer spending and purchasing of goods. This generally contributes to pollution of some kind from the production, transportation and eventual disposal of said goods. Consumption has costs for the environment. And modern economies, generally speaking, encourage a lot of consumption.

But it's not just environmentalists who display hypocrisy. Examples abound. Take our use of natural resources for food and fiber. Animal agriculture itself offers many opportunities for hypocrisy. Farm animals raised for food production, especially the quintessential horse, pig, cow, sheep and chicken, are often very relatable to people who are not directly involved in farming. Agricultural images featuring barns and landscapes are common, and those landscapes are dotted with the aforementioned animals. Cropping systems, such as corn and soybeans, remain in the background. Ask a three-year-old child to draw you a pig. You will get some variation on a circular figure colored pink. Ask the same child to draw a soybean plant and see what you get; your guess would be as good as mine.

This relatability to animals, despite possibly never having met that animal face-to-face, begins very early in life. Many children possess at least one, or many more than one, stuffed animals of some kind. But very few children are found sleeping with their cherished stuffed soybean. Beloved classics such as <u>Charlotte's Web</u> and <u>Stuart Little</u> by E. B. White introduce children to animals as their friends and confidants. Animals in media are often presented as children's friends and protectors. They are frequently defined as fiercely loyal, genuinely kind and with positive emotional appeal. One cannot forget the various dangerous situations which *Lassie* (the fictional dog character created by Eric Knight who stars in her own television series) and *Flipper*, the beloved television star bottlenose dolphin, traversed to help the children in their care.

<u>The Cat in the Hat</u> by Dr. Seuss is famous the world over. He has carried decades of children (and adults, perhaps) through adventures in books, and even on television. The book <u>Winnie the Pooh</u> has inspired much attention. He, along with his pals from the Hundred-Acre-Wood, have been friends to children since 1926. Pooh Bear, as his friends call him, is prominently featured in books, plush toys, clothing and on video. Perhaps the most undisputable evidence of Pooh Bear's fame is that the rights to Winnie-the-Pooh were licensed to Walt Disney Productions. Pooh Bear and his friends remain the feature characters at The Crystal Palace in Magic Kingdom at Walt Disney World Resort in Orlando, Florida, a testament to their fame and prominence in popular culture (and perceived economic potential).

Consider the peculiar case of revered rodents. We cherish memories of our first read of <u>Stuart Little</u>. And who among us does not love the internationally recognized poster-mouse of family fun and childhood wonder (and perhaps even magic), Mickey Mouse? So love Mickey Mouse, but now go set traps for the mouse (likely not a famous mouse, but a mouse nonetheless) in your house.

Bears, cats, mice and a whole lot of talking, feeling and emotion-laden farm animals have warmed our hearts for generations. Yet, many of the stars of such media are also features of the dinner table. They are our beloved friends and heroes on one hand, but on the other? Most of us don't have even a second thought of serving them up for dinner.

Basically, everyone's a hypocrite when you get down to it. Someone seeking to save the forest from being cut down, yet has wood furniture in their home is, yes, being hypocritical to some degree. The environmentalist who dares to heat his home is being hypocritical to some degree. And, the animal lover who hugs her puppy while eating a pork chop is also being hypocritical to some degree.

It's the way it is. And heaving insults at one another is unlikely to change anything, let alone create positive change. That path has been tried *many* times before. It's time to stop name-calling (what a hypocrite!) and focus on what can be done to improve our own personal situation, lessen our impact or move towards exemplifying our stated values, morals or ethics through our personal behaviors. Because we are *all* hypocrites at the end of the day. You, me and that environmentalist down the road.

If we can get over that, and move on to discerning how our actions can move the needle in the right direction, we may see positive change. We can't keep using the hypocrisy of others as a veil for why we shouldn't seek to do anything productive. Positive actions are positive and they should be encouraged out of our internal drive or moral obligations. *Even though* we, or they, are likely still hypocrites anyway.

Chapter 18: Bruce's Three Truths

The Timber Wars were painful, but educational. We learned a lot about leading the discussion over our future. Perhaps the most important things we learned, however, were three fundamental truths about engaging the public or our leaders around an issue.

These lessons are:

Democracy works, but it is not a spectator sport

For decades now, I have travelled and spoken across rural America. When it comes to politics, there is one comment I hear more than any other: the cities 'run' the politics of our state. Oregonians feel as if it is only Portland that has the number of voters needed to change elections. In Nebraska, the rural folks complain about Omaha and Lincoln. Coloradans whine about Denver dictating state politics. Montanans grumble about Billings (they have an escalator and that makes them a city...). Everywhere, I hear friends and family complain that with only 20 percent of the population living in rural areas, the 80 percent who live in the city dictate policy through the election process.

While there is an element of truth to this sentiment, the hand wringing misses an important fact about living in a participatory republic. We have what is essentially a binary political form where two parties share the support of the majority of the population relatively evenly. In this system, political muscle can be generated very successfully when there is a coalescing voice over a single issue.

Single issue, multi-sector voting blocs can, and often do, form during election cycles. They become what is widely known as the 'swing vote.' I learned this lesson when I participated in college student government politics and lobbied for students in Washington, DC. Students are a definite minority of the population, but we became a 'hard to ignore' voting bloc when we stood together. The same principle can be put to work for rural minorities.

Our 'single issue' can be broadly seen as environmental policy changes needed to protect the environment and economy of rural America. The multi-sector blocs are those of us in rural natural resource cultures such as farming, ranching, mining, logging, fishing and energy development.

Certainly, only 20 percent of our national population lives in rural areas. But that 20 percent represents the possibility of tens of millions of rural voters standing together to make the 'difference' in close elections. In individual states, that same math yields numbers like 100,000 rural voters in Montana where elections are generally decided by ten to twenty thousand votes.

I've seen it happen. During the election cycle of 2000, we decided to exercise the concept of the swing vote in Montana. During national campaigning the prior year, Representative Kennedy of Rhode Island was quoted as saying he had "written off" America's rural voters. He believed the party didn't need rural areas to win either the White House or the legislative branch races. When I read that quote, I was upset. I could only imagine the public outcry if any other minority segment of our population had been 'written off' by a major party.

So Tammy Johnson and I organized the rural vote in

Montana. We chose important races upon which to focus our attention, including the governorship, chief justice of the Montana Supreme Court, our federal legislative races and others. Our goal was to have 85 percent of our rural eligible voters show up at the polls. On the night of the election, the eastern media centers called most of our races by midnight – and we had lost the five races we were most concerned about.

However, we were having a blizzard in eastern Montana and our rural ballots were literally being driven to court houses in snow plows. By two in the morning, the election results on our five races were reversed. We had won each race by a 52 to 48 percent margin and our rural turnout was at 86 percent.

While I use the Democratic party line in this example, most of us know that in rural areas party lines largely fall apart. Most people in rural areas do not care if a person is running as a member of the Pajama Party. What is important to us is whether or not someone understands our issues, and is willing to stand with us if we stand with them.

Being informed on issues, candidates and voting is the centerpiece of making the political process work. I strongly encourage people to make sure that they vote, that they encourage their family member to vote and, if they have employees, they give time off for the voting process. *It is that important.*

There are many other ways to engage in the political process. Running for office is an option for those who are inclined. For rural areas, the offices that hold possibly the most influence over our future are local positions on planning boards, water boards, conservation boards, county commissions, city councils and school boards. Our local elected bodies represent our last line of defense in trying to ensure that policy being worked out at the ground level actually makes sense for the ground, and the people who live in the area.

I applaud all who make the decision to run for office. My oldest son, Chas, is one such person. He wanted desperately to be a logger and entered the School of Forest Engineering at Oregon State soon after graduating high school. At the end of his freshman year, however, he was told by the school that for them to have a good chance of placing him upon graduation, he should take a foreign language class. They suggested either Russian or Portuguese. In other words, the school felt the future of forest engineering was going to be strong in areas like Siberia and the Amazon of Brazil. He wanted to log in the Pacific Northwest.

So he came home and logged for a year. Then he reentered school at the University of Montana. During this time, he decided politics would have more to do with saving forest management in our nation than forestry, so he got his bachelor's degree in political science. Once graduated, he ran for office and was elected twice as our area's state representative. He's now finishing his second term as our state senator. The difference he's made to our state policy discussion will impact our forests and our forest families for generations to come. I could not be prouder of him or his accomplishments.

Yet most of us have no desire to toss our hat in the political ring. We need to entertain other ways of engaging in politics. We can and should do things like support candidates with individual or Political Action Committee contributions, volunteer our time in door-knocking for those we support, volunteer time doing political party work, post the names of those we support on our vehicles and in our yards, send thank you notes to leaders who take courageous positions for us and attend political debates and gatherings.

I find it interesting that we are sometimes hesitant to do something like pound someone's name in our yard because of the reaction we may get from those supporting another candidate or position. The irony of this hesitancy is that we fully expect those who we elect to have the courage to climb out on a political limb for us and our issues, and to do so even with the full illumination of the media.

We must stand up for those we support in politics if we want them to stand up for us and our policy positions. We must let those who are elected know that there is a constituency ready and able to applaud good decisions, and also ready to hold people accountable for bad decisions.

When people lead, leaders follow

The majority of those elected to a local, state or federal office have the same world view as the rest of society. Fewer and fewer elected positions are filled by those with a background in natural resource management such as agriculture or mining or forestry. Like the rest of society, they generally are rightfully concerned about the state of our environment, but have little real, direct or practical personal experience upon which to base their policy positions. This reality means that if we want good things to happen in policy discussions, we must accept the responsibility of offering solutions to the problems we face.

Through the early years of the Timber Wars, we did an outstanding job of whining and complaining about our current realities and the failures of current forest management policy. It finally dawned on us that we would not move forward unless we had policy solutions that we could offer to our leaders.

In preparation for President Clinton's Timber Summit held soon after he was elected, a group of grassroots leaders from the forest communities of the west spent over a year crafting a framework for policy discussions in our attempt to move forward in forest management on public lands. We listened to the public. We heard from them that they wanted a healthy forest ecosystem. We, too, wanted that long-term outcome. And so, we used it as the centralizing theme for a sweeping Vision Document.

Our Vision Document outlined the need to have forest management policy changes that would yield healthy forest ecosystems that coexisted with healthy social and economic systems. The solutions we sought would be socially acceptable, economically beneficial, biologically responsible and in concert with natural laws. We took the document to local elected leaders and opinion leaders and presented it to President Clinton at the Timber Summit with over half a million people's signatures of support.

Nothing happened with our document during the Clinton administration. But it gave us a positive foundation upon which to reengage the public. We could discuss the choices society faced in forest management. We were arguing 'for' a position and a vision we supported, rather than arguing 'against' someone else's position and vision.

Some of what we included in our Vision Document, and some of the policy discussion that followed, gave a lot of our supporters heartburn in those early days. We had to address some hard facts. We needed to not only ask the public to change their view of forest management, but we needed to change some of our long held traditional practices in order to get the public to support us. We needed to adopt and use some of the language that was socially accepted, not easily defined and very easily abused, terms such as 'sustainable forestry,' 'biological diversity' and 'ecosystem management.' But we knew that if we did not try to begin to define these terms within the policy discussion in a way that made sense, then we would have to live with the definition that others assigned them.

We also had to recognize that some of our practices, ones that made ecological sense, were tough to understand and needed to be abandoned. For instance, clear cutting of public forest lands (removing all of the trees in a given area) was long used as a proper forest management technique. Foresters who were faced with a two-hundred-acre patch of dead trees due to bug infestations would remove the stand and start over with new seedlings. The public, however, did not and does not like to look at what their eyes tell them is 'scorched earth.' Clear cutting is ugly, even if it is the right thing to do for the forest. Since we were largely unable to convince the public that clear cutting was sometimes good, we had to agree to strict limitations on its use as a technique. Any historic or traditional forest management technique that we found to be acceptable, but was not acceptable to the public, had to be modified.

The forest health discussion gained traction in the Bush administration. With a great deal of broad-based, bipartisan support, President George W. Bush signed into law the Healthy

Forest Restoration Act (HFRA). It is possibly the most progressive forest legislation passed since Teddy Roosevelt's days. We are nearly a decade past the signing of this law and progress is slow. But I firmly believe that our Vision Document, the HFRA that followed and our emphasis on local broad-based stakeholder collaboration has opened the door to hope for my grandchildren's forests and forest communities.

None of this would have happened if we didn't recognize that our future was going to be defined by a vision – either ours, or someone else's. We took on the responsibility. We shoved it into the light of public and political dialogue with hopes that our leaders would be led to good, sound policy decisions under which we and our forests could thrive.

The world is run by those who show up

Every single day of every single week of every single year, there are discussions being held over the future of rural America. The discussion might be at a planning board meeting, a water district hearing, a county commission meeting, a legislative hearing, in a school classroom, on the editorial page of a local newspaper or simply in a Facebook or Twitter post. If we want our voice and our position to be heard and, just as importantly, if we want to hear what others are saying and feeling, we need to respectfully participate in these discussions.

It is easy to let discussions slide on past, then complain about the outcome. It takes energy and focus to engage in these discussions. We have to listen and share and advocate for our vision and our solutions. I have long asked people, those who work in any field of natural resource management, to carve out some time during their busy work week to dedicate to 'showing up.' In fact, our business plans should include a new line item specifically for 'activism' (or being engaged in the process). At least one hour each week should be dedicated to that new line item.

The word 'activism' does not always make rural folks feel all warm and fuzzy. I often get a slightly frightened stare from audiences when I make the business line item request. I also recall the look my father gave me when I told *him* we needed to do that with Vincent Logging. Dad was in the shop welding on a dozer. I came through the bay doors with a newspaper in my hand. The newspaper had a headline story indicating a lawsuit had been filed that would shut down over one-third of the forest harvesting on our local public lands. I looked at Dad and told him that, in order to survive, we were going to have to become 'activists.'

He stood, flipped his welding helmet up and stared at me with a smoking welding rod in his right hand. His look told me he was trying to wrap his mind around growing hair down to his butt and smoking pot. I am sure he was also thinking that maybe a business-ending auction was a better solution than becoming 'activists.'

Think of activism as 'engagement.' The spirit of the word, in this context, is not what we have come to associate with it. Rather, it refers to the process of engaging in what is going on around you. Activism is not just holding marches and carrying pickets. These things may have their place when necessary, but the real work of engagement comes from putting ourselves in positions to work on the truths that we learned in the Timber Wars. It means dedicating time and resources to the political process, registering someone to vote, attending a political debate, phoning a county commissioner or sending an email to a senator or city council member. It means dedicating time and resources to leading our leaders by volunteering to work on our industry association committees, which are trying to form and promote policy that works for us and is acceptable to the public. It means dedicating time and energy to communicating our human story.

Chapter 19: Hunger for a New Vision

America is ready for a new environmental vision for our nation and the world. Most of society understands that humans have a role to play in protecting the environment and, though many may be misguided or misinformed, most would claim to be environmentally aware.

All too often, however, that awareness has been gained by a constant and relentless tsunami of fear. Since childhood, messages of doom about our planet have been packaged in movies, television shows, documentaries and news designed to scare individuals into taking action.

Often the action being requested is simple: write a check so that you can go about your normal life knowing you did your part to save the planet. As environmental issues are not usually front and center in people's lives, a prompt, easy-to-perform act such as the writing of a check alleviates a sense of personal responsibility. Groups built on conflict make billions of dollars each year on this premise.

Decades of fear-mongering has certainly worked. But the cracks are starting to show. People are tired of being scared and tired of the constant background noise. The doom-and-gloom, bongo-drum-beating, planet-is-dying message has exhausted many and caused others to just tune out the noise.

I get the feeling this hand has been overplayed when I speak at gatherings that are not natural resource centered. I have been invited to keynote the American Banking Association's annual meeting. Bankers were and are concerned about what is going on in the wealth creating sectors of natural resources and wanted to hear a message from a real person with real, ground-based experience. I have keynoted the National Association of Counties annual meeting, the Chambers of Commerce of West Las Vegas, Grand Rapids, Michigan, and elsewhere along with a host of elected leader gatherings in several states, provinces and countries.

Society seems to be searching for an alternative environmental message. Nowhere have I found the desire for a new message more vibrant than the groups of students who are attending academic institutions. My first real clue came when I was asked by the student president of Illinois State University in Bloomington to come and address the student population on Earth Day. My immediate reaction was, 'they want a logger to address them on Earth Day? They must be looking for someone to kill.' But I will speak to anyone, anywhere. I said I would be delighted. When I arrived at the auditorium, it was clear that some students had looked me up online. They were prepared to challenge me. There were picketers lining the back of the room with some signs that were, well, less than complimentary.

I started my presentation like I start every campus event, by sharing a little of my history as a student leader in college in the early 1970s. My generation of students asked tough questions of authority figures and demanded answers that made sense to us. I asked the students not to repeat the mistake my generation of student leaders made. When some of us decided we had discerned the only answers that mattered, we promptly traded asking questions for telling people what we demanded they accept as absolute truth. Universities are supposed to teach students 'how' to think, not 'what' to think, and I encouraged the students to be inquisitive of all information shared with them from their peers, their instructors and certainly from invited guests such as me.

The message I shared was the message I have shared for years: 'The old environmental movement was timely and necessary but failed to mature beyond a three-word vision of "Stop Doing That." This old vision is not going to work for their generation, particularly when they are sharing Planet Earth with between 9 and 11 billion other souls. Those people are going to need food, clothing and shelter. The issue facing their generation is not, 'are we going to manipulate the environment to meet the needs of humanity?' but rather, 'where, how and by whom?' are the processes of production to take place. This vision needs to be grounded in hope instead of fear, science instead of emotion, education instead of litigation and resolution instead of conflict. It must employ, rather than destroy, human resources.

I further suggested that the new environmental movement is going to be led by rural people. We live too close to the ground to pretend we know all the truth. But we are close enough to the ground to apply science and both provide from and protect the earth.

The reaction from the students was not what I had expected. After my concluding remarks they stood, clapped, whistled and stomped. As they finished their ovation, I was surprised to see them engage the picketers in the back of the room. They set their signs against the back wall or left. As everyone was getting reseated, I asked the student president what had just happened, admitting I felt like my part of the day's celebration was to present someone the students could 'boo' off the stage.

The response spoke volumes about where the next generation is coming from. He said, "We are tired of hearing that the planet *your* generation is handing us is a piece of crap. You gave us hope."

After leaving Illinois, I spoke that same week at both Dartmouth and Brown University as part of an Earth Day swing. The reaction was the same at each campus. The students were hungry, no, they were starving, to hear that there is real hope for them and their place on earth. They were hungry to hear a new vision of environmentalism.

The students are not alone. They are no different than the rest of society who will not, and I believe should not, embrace an anti-environment message but who are also searching for and willing to engage in a new environmental vision and body of leadership. That desire represents a door of opportunity for rural cultures. We can prepare our message of ground-based environmental realism, including resource management and commodity production that satisfies the very real needs of a growing population and takes care of planet earth.

We need the general population to engage with us in a constructive manner. They must trust that what we are sharing is the truth as best we know it. They often want transparency of our actions so they or a surrogate of theirs can confirm our words are being matched by our actions.

I am often asked a simple question at the end of my presentations: 'What can I do to help?' I have learned, over the years, that the answer is crucial because many have tried to 'help' and have accomplished the opposite. I now use H.E.L.P. as an acronym for a process that yields a position of leadership in this discussion over the environment:

H: Humanize

The dehumanization of our resource industries has long been an important part of campaigns centered around conflict. When a demanded policy change will devastate a segment of our rural cultural fabric, it is much easier to push for these policy changes if the humans being impacted are hidden behind a cloak of capital 'I' Industry, or are marginalized from the normal considerations of civil discourse.

In resource production, the humans (the little 'i' that inhabits the mythical corporate flow-charts) are hidden under all-encompassing terms that reflect not people, but business. Big business. Big, inhuman, heartless, profit-driven, anti-environment industry. In the Timber Wars, the conflict industry was not battling family logging companies and our rural forest communities. They referred to their 'opponent' as the large, multinational timber beasts. Our interests were consistently paired with the likes of Weyerhaeuser, Champion International or International Paper. The forest needed protecting not from 'people' but from mythical flow-charts in the sky.

Dehumanization works well. Society does not celebrate the success of industry like they did in earlier days. Industry is neither believed nor is it trusted. Conflict-oriented groups present themselves as the protagonist for real 'people' pitched in battle against a multitude of uncaring industrial antagonists. Terms such as 'factory farm,' 'agri-business,' 'industrial farming' and 'industrial forestry' are all used liberally with full knowledge that this positions them as the good guys against the bad.

We can fight against what we see as unfair or unjust in wrapping our rural culture in the trappings of multi-national corporations. Or we can accept that, for the time-being, social norms make it easy to vilify 'industry' and we must find a way to engage the public in a way that humanizes our efforts. The only way to successfully combat this knee-jerk negative reaction by the public is to present them with a human face.

We must cultivate ambassadors for our message of environmental hope and those ambassadors must have the potential to be believed and trusted by the public. These ambassadors need to be those of us in rural populations trying to reconnect with a public who can give or take our social license to operate. This is me, you, our family, our employees and possibly those indirectly attached to us or our industry through real relationships.

We cannot rely upon the representatives from our collective 'associations' to carry our water for us. Too often they can be written off by the public as 'industry hacks.' Our associations can assist us by arming us with information, but we must be the messengers that carry that information to the questioning public.

In the old days, people shared information with each other around kitchen tables, over backyard fences and through other face-to-face encounters. These interactions, with people to whom there is a relationship that fosters trust, provided the information (right or wrong) upon which opinions were constructed. Today, those same rules of opinion formation are at work – but often, although not always, the new backyard fences are online or through social media platforms. We can complain about this reality, or embrace the tools being used by society. I suggest we buck up and embrace.

E. Empathize

When we do embrace the public, whether a person next to us on a plane or a business peer at that Chamber of Commerce meeting, we need to remember what we in the timber industry had trouble with early on – empathize. Empathizing does not mean agreeing, it means listening, trying to see the world through the lens of their life and lifestyle and allowing them the right to an opinion (even if we think it is wrong).

Everyone, including each of us in rural America, constructs our beliefs, values and opinions based upon our experiences in the social and economic framework within which we live. Whether that body of world experience reflects the truths we believe to be sacrosanct doesn't really matter. What each person perceives to be true is, in fact, true – for them. Therefore, we must listen carefully to what a person is saying and try to understand their expressed concerns or opinions. We must try to discern how and why they have come to the conclusions they are expressing. We must value their opinions and expressed concerns as we would hope they will value our own opinions and our expressed concerns. If we don't want to listen and understand the position of someone, how can we expect them to listen and understand our position?

Only when we listen and understand how a person has reached the conclusion they are expressing can we begin to construct our answer. Only when we listen with respect to a person and hear what they are saying can we determine how we can construct a solution to that real or perceived problem that is 'acceptable.' This point is critical for each of us who works in a natural resource managing culture. It sets the framework for the public that says: "I am listening, I understand, I respect or I share your concerns and I am part of the answer to those concerns."

This can't happen without a great deal of introspection. It must be made in good faith and must be backed up with transparent actions that can be seen, measured and confirmed as 'solutions' by the public. It may require the construction of a third party certification to assure the public that we are not just moving our lips but are taking action.

Earlier I discussed the issue of water and forest practices in Montana. As mentioned, in the timber industry in Montana we developed a set of guiding principles for managing forests around stream courses and riparian areas. The public expressed concern that logging practices were negatively impacting our stream and the aquatic life that Montanans treasure. So we responded. And in doing so, we had to give up some long-standing production practices to meet the new standards that we set for ourselves. We also had to give up some practices that we thought made environmental sense but could not be clearly communicated to the public as sound.

Asking the public to 'believe us' wasn't going to work, so we constructed a process where a panel of independent experts from academia, non-governmental organizations (NGOs) and state and federal managing agencies travel from logging job to logging job doing surprise inspections and giving us a scorecard based upon meeting, exceeding or failing our standards. After years of operating within this framework, we can proudly face the public and, with third party certification, claim that we meet or exceed the standards set to protect their interest in Montana's waterways on over 99 percent of our operations. Some years our goal of 100 percent compliance is reached, and there is great peer pressure exerted on each of us to not be 'the operation' that yields the imperfect score. We took a big fundraising arrow out of the quiver of the conflict industry and broke it over our collective knees.

The national timber industry has moved toward a similar construct in answering the public's concern. A set of guidelines and standards that define 'sustainable forestry' are now part of a third-party certification program that yields 'Sustainable Forestry Initiative' (SFI) compliant forestry and logging operations. Foresters and loggers throughout the nation must now complete yearly training to assure that they are meeting the standards required of an SFI certified operation.

There are some practices that we needed to change and, importantly, as new information becomes available through the application of science, we will continue to modify our operations. Each year we must do a better job of listening to the public, hearing their concerns and constructing solutions to those expressed concerns that are acceptable to the public.

E. Educate (yes, a second 'E')

Once we have listened to the public and empathized with them about their real or perceived concerns, we can begin to undertake the process of educating. I often hesitate to use the term 'educate,' however, because it seems to draw up a mental picture of a 'student' and a 'teacher.' And, naturally, we want to be the teacher. Education, for us, must not be undertaken in a student/teacher format. What we must do to 'educate' the public is 'share' with them how we can be part of the solution to what they think is a problem. Sharing is a bit different than educating in that it is a two-way street: we listen and hear what the public is saying and we ask that they give us that same respect.

It simply does not work to forcibly educate others. Forcibly educating other adults is generally more like attacking than sharing, and is met with the expected departure of your intended pupil more often than not.

It does us no good to spend enormous amounts of time and energy answering questions we think the public needs answered. This pertains to one of the many lessons we learned the hard way. We thought 'science' was the trump card that would give the public all they needed to support us. The public, however, was having emotional reactions to our complex issues. Throwing white papers at them did very little good. We certainly needed the science. But we needed to learn to package the science in terms that the public both understood and could support.

This piece of the puzzle was incredibly important in constructing the basis for federal timber management through legislation. We heard what the public wanted: a healthy, sustainable forest. We gathered the science needed to achieve that goal and then packaged the discussion in terms that the public could understand, accept and emotionally support. The final legislative package became known as the Healthy Forest Initiative. This public land management signed into law by President George W. Bush. It is not a panacea and it will take years to fully implement, but it is a light at the end of a decades-long tunnel.

Because we have listened to the public and are trying to solve our shared problems, we've moved beyond entrenched battles with local conservationists. We have, for over twenty years, worked locally in collaborative efforts. Local stakeholders who were, in the past, combatants in our Timber Wars, now sit at a common table of debate. Our local efforts are often shot down by regional or national environmental conflict groups still raising money by filing lawsuits against the federal government and getting paid under the Equal Access to Justice money stream. These entities are, however, now being marginalized by the real conservationists with whom we are working towards resolution and solutions. We have made a host of unlikely friends who we trust, and who trust us. Our common problem is those who are committed not to the future of the forest but to the future of their bottom line.

In moving beyond combat and working on 'sharing' solutions with the public, we also had to work on how we presented ourselves in the discussion. It was common to hear, in conversations between individuals and in groups of hundreds or thousands, the common refrain that 'we are the true environmentalists.' That statement was often sandwiched in between tirades against the conflict industry in which we cursed those 'damned environmentalists,' or 'stupid tree-huggers,' or 'ignorant greenies.' We need to let this type of language go the way of the dodo bird.

When sharing over the backyard fence, it's okay to be green! In fact, it is required. The public self-identifies with the 'greenies' and they consider themselves to be one of those 'environmentalists' we are damning. We must be the leaders of the environmental discussion and be proud to be green. In fact, to ultimately get the public to endorse us and our actions, we must 'out-green' the 'posers' from within the industries thriving on continued dissention. We must be the 'green' answer to the public's 'environmental' concerns. We cannot claim to be the leader of the environmental discussion when we identify that group as bastards. If it seems commonsense not to name-call and disparage others whom you wish to lead, that's because it is.

L: Lead Locally

We are a huge nation. There are over 300,000,000 stakeholders in this discussion of the environment. How, I asked myself, are we ever going to reach all those people? While I was pondering this ugly reality, a family from Kettle Falls, Washington, sent me a copy of a quiz taken by their second-grade daughter in the elementary school of their small timber town. The quiz was on dinosaurs and included five questions. Four of the questions concerned the science of dinosaurs.

One of the five questions, however, was clearly out of place. It asked students to circle the 'person who endangers animals.' The choices were a small girl with a cat, a boy with a dog, a man watching ponies in a pen, a scientist working in a laboratory....and a logger working in the forest. The father who sent me the quiz expressed three valid concerns. First, the quiz was supposedly about dinosaurs and included four questions about them and then one question that simply bashed on loggers. Second, the quiz should not have been given to students nationwide in a scholastically accepted curriculum. Third, his second-grade daughter should not have received a 'good job' mark on the paper because she correctly circled the logger. The man who sent the quiz to me was a forester for Boise Cascade.

This example, which I still carry in my briefcase as a harsh reminder, drove home the point that we do not begin our conversation and relationship building in some far off city. We begin at home. In our living room. In our neighborhood. In our local civic groups. In our local schools. We should not worry about the opinion page of the *Chicago Tribune* more than the opinion page of the *Kootenai Valley Record.*

Those who live in our local communities get the same two hundred channels of bad news as those who live in New York City. If they do not have a direct connection to the ground-based realities of our resource industries, they have every chance of being just as disconnected from what we know to be true as the people residing in a faraway (or nearby) city. Therefore, our efforts to listen, to hear, to share and to construct solutions must not begin in a place far away. The backyard fence that first warrants our attention is the one in *our own backyard.*

The elected leaders we should be most concerned about are also those from close to home. County Commissions, City Councils, Conservation and Water Boards, Zoning Boards and other locally-elected bodies are filled with people who may or may not have a resource rich background. Yet they can have a huge impact on our management operations. Further, our locally-elected bodies are our last line of defense in keeping bad policy from compromising our ability to stay in business. They can become some of our greatest ambassadors in presenting alternatives to a concerned public. We must treat them with the same care as we treat other stakeholders. We must use the same tools of empathizing and sharing with them.

P: Participate

This refers to the need to set aside business hours to lead and engage in your rural culture. This duty to be an engaged citizen and participant in your own corner of the World cannot be assigned to someone else. It is our responsibility and it must be integrated into our business plans as surely as we integrate equipment maintenance. This is the way we answer the truth we learned about: the world is run by those who show up.

Certainly, the most important things done during business hours are those things that allow us to operate, make a profit and thus remain in business and providing for our own families and those that are served by our efforts. That reality must always inform our decisions. Not making a profit will assure that we do not have a business.

However, maintaining our social license and working to assure that we are operating in a manner that is acceptable to the public is, ultimately, as important as making a profit. We only operate with the consent of the public. Lose that consent and they remove our license to operate and our ability to yield a profit – and thus our ability to exist in business for ourselves, our employees (and their families) and our stakeholders.

What can you do? Add a line item to your business plan for engagement and dedicate time and capital resources to that line item. You do not need to single-handedly save your culture. But you should make a commitment to doing your fair share in leading the discussion that will define the future.

Each of us brings something different to the table in the way of skills, ambitions, interests and passions. Find something that 'turns your crank' and engage. See the Appendix for just a small sample of the many ways you can do this, along with some firsthand stories of how these different options have worked.

Be a ripple. Society is ready to hear a new vision of environmental stewardship that is based upon hope for humankind and our planet. We are learning how to do more than just fight over someone else's vision of our future. We are learning to articulate and share a vision of our own.

There are literally hundreds of things that you can do to become an advocate for your culture. You do not need to do hundreds of things. You need to commit to doing something. If each of us does this, there is every reason to have hope that there is a future for coming generations of natural resource managers in our great nation.

I tend to have trouble isolating single actions upon which to focus. I tend to try to eat an entire elephant in one bite, or get paralyzed when too many options are placed in front of me. My mom knew of this problem. Prior to losing her to cancer, she shared with me the following quote:

> *It is from numberless diverse acts of courage and belief that human history is shaped. Each time a man stands up for an ideal, or acts to improve the lot of others, or strikes out against injustice, he sends forth a tiny ripple of hope, and crossing each other from a million different centers of energy and daring, those ripples build a current that can sweep down the mightiest walls of oppression and resistance.*
> *— Bobby Kennedy, South Africa, 1966*

Each of us does not have to try to make a wave. Rather, we must be committed to making a ripple and *together* we will make a wave. Standing together, engaging a concerned public and offering a new environmental message of hope can save both the Last Best Places *and* the Last Best People.

Appendix: Potential Ways to Engage

There are numerous ways you might choose to engage in your community. Not every potential engagement opportunity offered will appeal to everyone. Further, not every opportunity is fitting for everyone. Consider the following options in the context of your own situation and be mindful of what you can and cannot do within the confines of your operation, your resources and your level of comfort.

1. Open your operation to tours for your community.

While there may be interest in the massive equipment you own and operate, the most important thing shared with visitors is not the machines – but the human face of those that operate the machines. Humanizing our industries begins at home, and tours offer mind-opening opportunities to listen and share.

2. Celebrate Earth Day.

Every year we dedicate an entire week to discussing the global environment. I once asked a large timber company if they ever dedicated any money to that event and they said, "yeah, we spend a lot of money on Earth Day." "Really?" I asked, "on what?" His response was telling: "We spend about a half million dollars a year on increased security."

Increased security might be necessary, but we should use the occasion to champion the good news about environmental progress. One year in Montana, farmers, ranchers, miners and loggers worked with our local Pizza Hut franchises so that each store gave away a tree seedling, a coloring book on how to plant the tree (and not kill it) and students from local schools went to logging jobs, farms, ranches and mines to deliver pizza to the workers and offer a thank you for 'doing a better job of protecting the environment every day.'

The news media across the state had one upbeat story that day and used the footage for a week. Earth Day should not be a day of gloom but should be a day to share and promote our message of progress and hope.

3. Deliver a presentation of your operation and your industry to local civic groups.

Local community members can be just as disconnected as urban dwellers if they do not currently work in a resource production occupation. Share your story and then listen carefully to hear the concerns of your local public. If you don't already belong to your local Chamber of Commerce, consider joining so that you can share your realities with local business peers.

4. Present to a classroom.

Our children need to meet a real person who works in the environments they love. Just because they live in a resource-dependent community does not assure that they know anything about the realities of farming, ranching, mining, logging, fishing or energy development. They, like their peers across the nation, get the same messages drilled into them through the Disney channel, cartoons, *Ranger Rick Magazine* and the ever-present *Weekly Reader*. They, like their peers, are incredibly interested in meeting a real person who does something cool like help bring food to their table or manage a forest.

Some years ago, I was doing my 'one hour per week' by going into schools and listening to the young students. At a school in the small timber town of Seeley Lake, Montana, the teacher thanked me for coming and said that it was timely for me to be there. The following day, a gal was coming into the classroom with a wolf. The kids were going to get to adopt the wolf, name it and track it for a year. During my 220 miles of windshield time going back home, I pondered what was going on in that classroom.

I knew the person bringing in the wolf and knew that she was going to assist the students in naming the wolf something like 'Alfred.' On the way out, she was going to hammer home her message that 'logging is bad for Alfred; farming is bad for Alfred; ranching is bad for Alfred.' What, I wondered, do we have to compete with this? The only thing I could come up with was: we have us. When I returned home, I called the teacher in Seeley Lake and told her I thought it was great that the kids were getting to adopt a wolf, but how would they like to adopt a logger? I told her I have a name and everything already, but they could adopt me, communicate with me for a year and then on Earth Day the next spring I could come visit with them again. The teacher thought the idea had merit. And the class adopted me. After the year was over and I had visited with the students again, the teacher was thrilled. She then asked if we could do it again and maybe broaden it to have the kids adopt a farmer or rancher or miner as well.

What was born in that little logging town was a program that ultimately grew to include students in cities such as New York, Los Angeles, Detroit, Little Rock and Minneapolis and small towns such as Pinedale, Wyoming, and Graves County, Kentucky. It is called Provider Pals. An opinion piece in *The Wall Street Journal* called it one of the most important outreach programs in the nation. Over 100,000 students have enjoyed meeting resource workers. The students and teachers are forever changed by the interaction with the human face of our industries. Those resource workers are similarly changed since the program is built upon 'sharing' realities and world views and serves as an introduction for our rural culture to the realities of urban living. We are aware that people residing outside our rural communities know little about who we are and what we do, but we also know precious little about the life and realities of our urban peers. Through an engagement of mutual learning and sharing, common ground can be found.

The first questions invariably asked by the students do not have anything to do with 'parts per million' or 'basil area per acre.' The first questions are tough ones like: 'How big is your truck?' 'What time do you get up?' 'Have you ever been chased by a bear?' 'Do you have any scars I can look at?' They want to know who we are long before they get to the questions about what we do.

You do not need to have a program or build a program to achieve these same results. You can and should engage your local schools in a similar fashion. Ask a teacher in your local elementary, middle or high school if they would like to engage in a cultural exchange with you. The clear majority of students and their teachers are thrilled to have the opportunity to meet us, talk with us, share with us and build mutual respect and understanding. Most resource industries have information designed to complement curricula in our schools and this information is incredibly important. The information contained in Ag in the Classroom or Project Learning Tree has immensely more value if, prior to delivery of the curricula, there is a human connection forged with the teachers and students.

5. Use social media.

Construct a Facebook site for your operation that can be shared with 'friends.' On your site, offer tidbits of information about you, your family, your operation and your pride in being an environmentally aware producer of 'stuff' the public needs and uses. Remember to 'empathize' before you try to 'forcibly educate' if someone shares a contrasting view on your page.

Consider the new 'live streaming' option available on Facebook or YouTube. Short, personalized videos of you at work in your operations can strike the same note as the one-hour docu-dramas that now populate prime time television (*Deadliest Catch*, *Ax Man*, etc). We are now so separated from society that many of our urban peers can't get enough of viewing us in our natural habitat.

Use Twitter to engage a following and share your positive news of hope as you learn ever more about your trade and the good news about what you do for the public and their environment.

6. Get out the welcome wagons.

I find it interesting that many rural areas treat newcomers with a great deal of disdain unless they are a relative or friend. In fact, we often treat newcomers like the enemy until a few weeks after they are dead. Newcomers feel this animosity deeply. My wife's first stop upon getting married was to the courthouse to get rid of her California driver's license because she was tired of getting grief every time she showed it for identification. The 'shut the door behind me, I am already here and no-one else is welcome' mentality was not always our way. In fact, in the old days we met newcomers with nothing short of glee. After all, newcomers meant new money, new ideas and someone besides a cousin to marry our daughter. We had welcome wagons that met the newbies and gave them a pie!

We need to resurrect that welcome party atmosphere. We cannot keep new people from coming into our areas. We can assume that the attraction they feel toward our 'places' are the same things that cause us to like calling our 'places' home. We should meet them, thank them for choosing to join our area, explain the proud history of the area and encourage them to become a part of our hopeful future. If we do not do this, I have seen where new people congeal into groups after being treated like an enemy, and then do begin to become the enemy within.

Our local chambers of commerce, realtors and churches generally meet newcomers first. Work with them to figure out how to 'welcome' your newest community members. Treat newcomers with respect and they may just become a positive ambassador for your community and your industry.

About the Authors

Bruce Vincent is a 3rd generation logger from Libby, Montana. Today, he is as a motivational speaker and travels the world presenting in front of diverse audiences. He often provides testimony on resource issues before Congress. Bruce has been reported on by *Outside*, *Wheat Life*, *Range*, *Tree Farmer*, *Time* and *Audubon* magazines as well as *The Wall Street Journal*, *New York Times*, *San Francisco Chronicle*, *Los Angeles Times*, *Washington Post* and others. He has appeared on "60 Minutes" and participated in radio shows, documentaries and broadcasts across the nation and several countries. Bruce was on the cover of *Evergreen Magazine* and included in William Perry Pendley's book It Takes A Hero.

Nicole J Olynk Widmar is an associate professor of agricultural economics at Purdue University in West Lafayette, Indiana. A native New Yorker, Nicole is an alumni of Cornell University (BS) and Michigan State University (MS and PhD). A thought leader in her field, she has notable presence, and significant followings, on GoogleScholar and ResearchGate. Nicole has over 65 peer-reviewed articles on consumer perceptions, animal welfare, technology adoption, production economics and other related areas. Nicole has published over 65 additional articles in various outlets including magazines and blogs, along with 24 podcasts. She is an up-and-coming forerunner on pressing social issues related to agriculture and rural America.

Jessica Eise is an Alaskan-born writer with expertise in communication, media, technology and food and agriculture. Now residing in Indiana, she is author of The Communication Scarcity in Agriculture. Jessica studied journalism at New York University (MA) and is experienced in media production, new media and journalism, having worked in these areas throughout Latin America, the Middle East, Africa and in Washington, DC. Learn more about Jessica at **www.jessicaeise.com** or on Twitter @JessicaEise.

Made in the USA
Lexington, KY
31 March 2017